Listening & Notetaking Skills

Without Audioscripts

Patricia A. Dunkel & Frank Pialorsi

With

Lynn Bonesteel
Miriam Espeseth
Daphne Mackey
Catherine Mazur-Jefferies

NATIONAL
GEOGRAPHIC
LEARNING

HEINLE
CENGAGE Learning

Australia • Brazil • Japan • Korea • Mexico • Singapore • Spain • United Kingdom • United States

Listening and Notetaking Skills 3,
Fourth Edition
Without Audioscripts

Patricia A. Dunkel and Frank Pialorsi

Publisher: Sherrise Roehr

Executive Editor: Laura Le Dréan

Director of Global Marketing: Ian Martin

International Marketing Manager: Caitlin Thomas

Product Manager: Emily Stewart

Director, Content and Media Production:
Michael Burggren

Content Project Manager: Andrea Bobotas

Print Buyer: Mary Beth Hennebury

Cover Designers: Christopher Roy and
Michael Rosenquest

Cover Image: Bruno De Hogues/Getty Images

Compositor: Page Designs International

For product information and technology assistance, contact us at
Cengage Learning Customer & Sales Support,
1-800-354-9706

For permission to use material from this text or product,
submit all requests online at **www.cengage.com/permissions**.
Further permissions questions can be e-mailed to
permissionrequest@cengage.com.

Student Book ISBN: 978-1-305-49344-5

National Geographic Learning
20 Channel Center Street
Boston, MA 02210
USA

Cengage Learning is a leading provider of customized learning solutions with office locations around the globe, including Singapore, the United Kingdom, Australia, Mexico, Brazil and Japan.

Cengage Learning products are represented in Canada by Nelson Education, Ltd.

Visit National Geographic Learning online at **ngl.cengage.com.**

Visit our corporate website at **www.cengage.com.**

Printed in the United States of America
Print Number: 02   Print Year: 2017

CONTENTS

SCOPE AND SEQUENCE

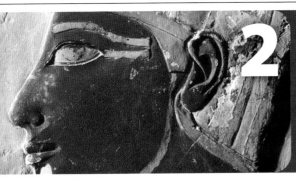

Notetaking Preparation	Expansion	Unit Video
• Recording Important Information	**Reading:** Vikings Filed Their Teeth, Skeleton Study Shows	The Gift of Traveling 
• Recording Information as a List	**Reading:** Last of the Cave People	
• Recording Numbers and Dates in Notes	**Reading:** Ramses the Great	Palenque 
• Using Indentation and Spacing Effectively in Notes	**Reading:** Terra-Cotta Army Protects First Emperor's Tomb	
• Using Intonation to Identify New Main Points	**Reading:** "Second Life," Other Virtual Worlds Reshaping Human Interaction	An Actor and a Travel Writer 
• Showing Cause and Effect	**Reading:** Why Are Young, Educated Americans Going Back to the Farm?	
• Recording Rhetorical Questions	**Reading:** Love that Lingua Franca	Digital Nomad 
• Contrast Cues and Charts	**Reading:** Smarter Teams Are More Sensitive, Have More Women?	
• Anticipating and Recording Examples	**Reading:** Genes and Population Genetics	The Human Journey 
• Vocabulary: Recovering Meaning as You Listen	**Reading:** Food: How Altered?	

UNIT WALKTHROUGH

New to This Edition

- Authentic **National Geographic videos** provide a meaningful context for discussion and application of essential listening, notetaking, and vocabulary skills.

- New and updated **academic lectures** offer compelling, cross-curricular content that simulate authentic scenarios for maximum academic readiness.

- Every unit introduces a focused aspect of **notetaking** and provides varied opportunities for practice and application of the skill.

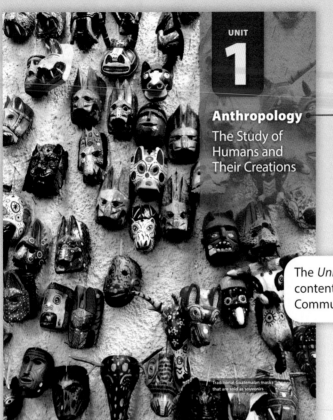

UNIT 1

Anthropology
The Study of Humans and Their Creations

Traditional Guatemalan masks that are sold as souvenirs

The *Unit Theme* focuses on an academic content area relevant to students' lives such as Communication, Biology, and Anthropology.

Before Listening activities prepare students for success by activating background knowledge and providing the language and skills necessary for comprehension.

CHAPTER 1

Anthropologists

Working in a Diverse Profession

Anthropologist, Dr. Lee Berger at an excavation site in Gladysvale, South Africa

2 Unit 1 • Anthropology

TOPIC PREVIEW

Answer the following questions with a partner or your classmates.

1. Look at the title of this unit. *Anthropos* is the Greek word for "man." What is anthropology?

2. Look at the title of this chapter. What different types of anthropologists do you think there are?

3. Do you think anthropology can tell us more about the past, the present, or the future? Explain.

BEFORE LISTENING

VOCABULARY PREVIEW

(A) Read through the sentences below, which are missing vocabulary from the lecture. Listen to the sentences and write the missing words in the blanks.

1. As Paul Bohannan, _____ anthropologist, pointed out a number of years ago. "Each science that deals with people has its own definitions of *human*."

2. Anthropology attempts to be _____—the study of human behavior in all places and throughout time.

3. Mostly the work of anthropologists is not _____ and involves repetitive and _____ activities.

4. In the modern day, anthropology is a _____ social science with two broad fields and several _____ or subfields.

5. _____ is the study of different cultures through material _____ rather than direct interviews or observations of the group under study.

6. _____, as you probably know, is the study of language as communication among humans.

7. Culture is learned and _____ primarily through language.

8. _____ is the _____ description of human societies, mostly based on firsthand fieldwork.

9. It is important to note that there are several _____ common among all societies.

10. So, you might ask, what are the practical _____ for such a broad field?

(B) Check the spelling of the vocabulary words with your teacher. Discuss the meanings of these words and any other unfamiliar words in the sentences.

PREDICTIONS

Think about the questions in the Topic Preview on page 2 and the sentences you heard in the Vocabulary Preview. Write three questions that you think will be answered in the lecture. Share your questions with your classmates.

Chapter 1 • Anthropologists 3

The *Notetaking Preparation* section presents a variety of effective notetaking techniques. Using content from the unit, students practice these techniques in authentic academic situations.

NOTETAKING PREPARATION

Recording Important Information

Efficient notetakers do not write down every word of a lecture. Here are some tips for taking notes:

- Listen for and note the main ideas of the lecture.
- Write only the key words, not complete sentences.
- Use abbreviations for common words or for a specific word that you hear many times in the lecture. There are many ways to abbreviate. Figure out what abbreviations make sense to you. Here are some examples:

  shorten long words to one or two syllables
  problem = prob   anthropology = anthro

  leave out the vowels
  problem = prb or prblm

  use a single letter for a high-frequency word
  Egypt = E   price = p

- When you miss something in the lecture, leave some space.
- After a lecture, go back and write out any words you abbreviated and might not remember later. Check with the lecturer or another student to fill in information you missed.

A Look at the abbreviations. Match the abbreviations to words from the lecture.

1. *devt*   _____ cultural
2. *comp*   _____ anatomy
3. *anat*   _____ development
4. *cult*   _____ subjects
5. *subj*   _____ comparative

6. *anthro*   _____ evolution
7. *phys*   _____ analysis
8. *As*   _____ physical
9. *evol*   _____ anthropologists
10. *anlys*   _____ anthropology

B Listen to sentences from the lecture. Take notes. Use abbreviations where possible.

1. _____
2. _____
3. _____
4. _____
5. _____

4   Unit 1 · Anthropology

Notetaking Skills

Throughout the *Listening & Notetaking Skills* series, learners develop a wide variety of notetaking strategies necessary for academic success. Learners are taught the essential principles of notetaking and encouraged to personalize the strategies for maximum results.

Listening sections introduce the academic lecture. Learners listen to the lecture three times, focusing on a different listening and notetaking skill with each repetition.

LISTENING

FIRST LISTENING

Listen to the lecture and number the slides on this page and the next in the order they would be shown during the lecture. Write the number of the slide on the line provided and answer the question to the right of the slide.

Coexistence of Culture and Society

Isolated cultures

Multicultural or pluralist

Subcultures

Slide # _____
What is an example of a pluralist society?
_____

A Particular Culture

A shared way of life
- Ways of thinking, acting, feeling
- Concrete things

Slide # _____
What are some concrete things that tell us about a particular culture?
_____

Similarities Across Cultures

Importance of discovering similarities

Universals among societies

The role of the individual

Slide # _____
How many "universals" among all cultures does the lecturer mention?
_____

Cultural Anthropology

Why study cultural anthropology?
- Fascinating story of cultural growth
- Learn and use a foreign language
- Intercultural understanding

Slide # _____
What is the definition of cultural anthropology?
_____

What Is Culture?

Murdock / Tylor / Kessing

Learned, socially transmitted behavior

Slide # _____
How many categories did Murdock list?
_____

14   Unit 1 · Anthropology

Chapter 2 · The Concept of Culture   15

After Listening sections provide learners with opportunities to discuss the lecture through pair and group activities.

ACCURACY CHECK

You will hear questions about the lecture. Answer each question by referring to the notes that you took while listening to the lecture.

1. a. Mead
   b. Tylor
   c. Murdock

2. a. savagery
   b. language
   c. barbarism

3. a. 1962
   b. 1989
   c. 1993

4. a. communication
   b. social variables
   c. empathy and curiosity

5. a. a remote tribe
   b. a pluralistic society
   c. people in a large city

6. a. civilization
   b. savagery
   c. multiculturalism

7. a. political
   b. military
   c. informal

8. a. Seelye
   b. Sapir
   c. Benedict

The *Oral Summary* asks learners to use their notes to reconstruct the content of the lecture.

ORAL SUMMARY

Use your notes to create an oral summary of the lecture with a partner. As you work together, add details to your notes that your partner included but you had missed.

DISCUSSION

Discuss the following questions with a classmate or in a small group.

1. After listening to the lecture, do you find *culture* difficult or easy to define? What is your definition? In what ways is it the same or different from definitions in the lecture?

2. List four or five cultural "generalizations" that foreigners may have about your country.

3. "If a group or society is small, isolated, and stable, it might also share a single culture." Do you know of any such "single" cultures in the world? What would you look for to decide if a group of people share a "single" culture?

Chapter 2 · The Concept of Culture **17**

Through guided prompts, *Discussion* activities provide opportunities for learners to hone communicative and critical thinking skills.

An *Expansion* section in each chapter includes high-interest National Geographic articles that present information related to the unit theme.

PRE-READING

The following Reading is about the experiences of an anthropological research team in the mountains of Papua New Guinea. Before you read, answer the following questions. Share your answers with a classmate.

1. Look at the title of the article and the photograph on the next page. Write two things that you expect to learn about the "Cave People" from the article.

2. In the lecture, the speaker discussed reasons to study cultural anthropology. Why would a team of researchers want to visit these people in Papua New Guinea?

READING

Now read the article.

Last of the Cave People
by Mark Jenkins

The vast geographic variation of Papua New Guinea created tremendous biological diversity, which in turn was accompanied by enormous cultural diversity. It is only in the most deeply inaccessible regions that enclaves of traditionally nomadic people, like the Meakambut, still exist. The Meakambut were unknown to the outside world until the 1960s. In 1991 anthropologist Borut Telban spent a week in the area and found only 11 Meakambut. When Telban returned in 2001, he couldn't locate them again.

In hopes of meeting up with these last semi-nomadic holdouts, an anthropological researcher named Nancy Sullivan sent out a team to find the Meakambut and inventory their caves. Sullivan's team discovered 52 surviving Meakambut and 105 caves with names.

Our team flies into the Sepik River basin. We skim up smaller and smaller tributaries in a motor dugout. Finally we strike out on foot into the mountains. We try reaching the Meakambut by jungle telephone: Three men pound the trunk of a towering tree with wooden bats. When this doesn't work, we set out on a two-day trek to the group's last known whereabouts.

At noon the next day, two Meakambut men come striding into our camp. They recognize Joshua Meraveka, a member of Sullivan's team. He introduces them as John and Mark Aiyo. John is a leader

of the Meakambut. While waiting there for the rest of the Embarakal to arrive, John explains cave life to me. He says they like their hunter-gatherer life and have no interest in changing it.

Before long, the rest of the Meakambut arrive. This is when we first encounter Lidia, curled up by the fire, coughing horribly. A member of our team, an emergency medical technician, examines Lidia. He determines that she likely has a life-threatening case of pneumonia and gives her double doses of antibiotics and Tylenol. We suggest that first thing in the morning she be carried out of the mountains, to a clinic in the village of Amboin. Two other Meakambut are also seriously ill.

One man from our team, Sebastian Haraha, is an ethnographer who has come to pinpoint the locations of the Meakambut's caves. He hopes to register them so the homeland of the Meakambut will be protected. Now, he volunteers to escort the sick.

Two nights later, John begins to let down his guard. He admits that his group hasn't eaten meat or killed a pig for over three months. He is deeply worried for his people. When the campfire dies out, John whispers something he wants me to pass on to the government of Papua New Guinea.

The next morning our team leaves the mountains. We reach our motor dugout and travel downstream

A member of the Meakambut tribe wearing bird-feather headdress

to the village of Awim and learn that Lidia and the others are here. Lidia is alive. Simple antibiotics have saved her.

At breakfast, I find Sebastian Haraha. "Protecting the caves? What does it matter if there are no Meakambut left?" asks Sebastian. "The Meakambut are on the edge of extinction. They are dying from easily treatable illnesses. In ten years they could be

completely gone, and their culture and language would vanish. When I get back to Port Moresby, I'm going to walk straight into the prime minister's office and do something."

I nod and pass along John's message: "We, the Meakambut people, will give up hunting and always moving and living in the mountain caves if the government will give us a health clinic and a school, and two axes and two shovels and two axes, so we can build homes."

The Meakambut continue to live without access to government services. But they have partly settled in homes on the ridgetop camp of Tembakapa. Despite the threat of encroachment by miners, they continue to hunt and gather on their traditional land.

DISCUSSION

Discuss these questions with a classmate.

1. What surprised or interested you most about the culture described in the passage? Why?

2. What was the role of the anthropologists in this story? How was it similar to or different from what you learned about anthropologists and ethnologists in the lecture?

3. What information from the lecture was exemplified in the article?

RESEARCH PROJECT

Individually or in a group, research one of the following topics. Write a short paper on the topic, or plan and present a group presentation to inform the class about the topic.

1. Isolated cultures: Where do they still exist, and what challenges do they face?

2. Research in cultural anthropology: What similarities and differences exist between your culture and another?

3. Intercultural understanding: Does studying or living in another culture change an individual's values? Provide evidence to support your opinion.

4. Another related topic that interests you or your group.

Additional expansion activities centered on the unit theme include online research, short essays, and classroom presentations for academic preparation.

Unit Video

Each unit ends with an authentic **National Geographic** video that is related to the unit theme. Most of the videos are in a lecture format, giving students a further opportunity to practice notetaking skills.

UNIT 1 VIDEO
The Gift of Traveling

BEFORE VIEWING

TOPIC PREVIEW

What do you think it would be like to be a professional photographer who travels around the world? Write some pros and cons of the job. Discuss your answers with a partner.

Pros	Cons

VOCABULARY PREVIEW

Ⓐ Read the definitions of these key words and phrases that you will hear during the video.

hanging out with spending leisure time with
flexibility the ability to easily adjust to new situations
had language in common shared the same language
set up camp find a new place to start a home and live
on assignment carrying out a job you are hired to do as a journalist or photographer
compelling so interesting that you want to pay close attention to it
immerse yourself become completely involved in something
abide by follow a particular law, custom, rule, etc.
inspirational making you feel excited and have creative ideas

Ⓑ Work with a partner and write in the blank the word from the box that completes the sentence.

| communities | culture | kids | photographers |
| spend | stories | travelers | unusual |

1. Annie's children travel with her to foreign countries and _____ a lot of time **hanging out with** _____ from other cultures.
2. When making friends in new _____, people don't always **have** the same **language in common**.
3. **Flexibility** is an important quality for professional _____ **on assignment** because they might have to **set up camp** in some _____ places.
4. Experienced _____ know that it is important to **abide by** the customs of the culture you are visiting.
5. You can **immerse yourself** in another _____, even if you can't speak the language.
6. When photographs are **compelling** and **inspirational**, it makes people want to read the _____ that accompany them.

VIEWING

📺 FIRST VIEWING

Watch the video, and then compare your first impressions with a partner. Talk about what you remember, what surprised you, and what interested you.

📺 SECOND VIEWING

Watch the video again. Listen for the missing words and write them in the blanks.

1. Our kids have traveled to every continent except _____. More importantly, when we travel they have lived in communities. We never stayed in _____.
2. But that if you go into each culture open, and look people in the _____ and observe and listen, you're going to make connections that are well beyond what most _____ get to see.
3. And so the real challenge for a photographer is to bring her or his own unique _____ to that subject _____.
4. The camera has always given me an _____ to walk up to people and spend time with them and even go _____ with them.

Listening and Notetaking Skills Series Components

The Audio CDs provide all the lectures and listening activities contained in the Student Book.

The Video DVD contains five authentic **National Geographic** videos relating to the units in the book.

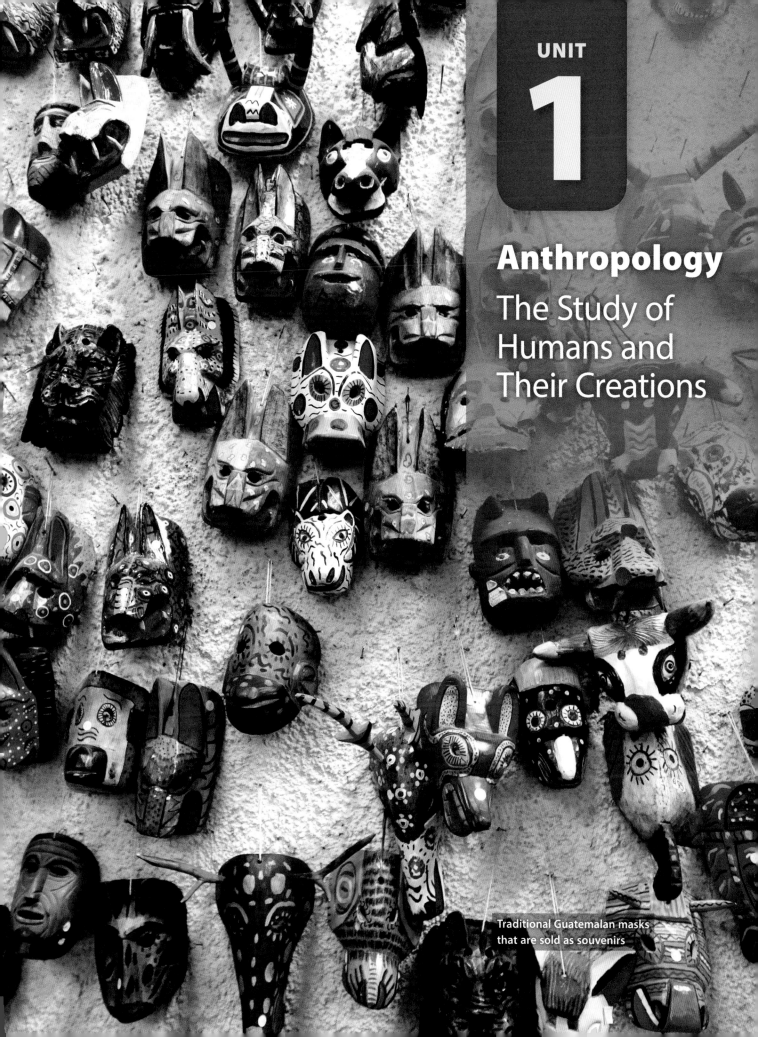

Anthropology
The Study of Humans and Their Creations

Traditional Guatemalan masks that are sold as souvenirs

Anthropologists

Working in a Diverse Profession

TOPIC PREVIEW

Answer the following questions with a partner or your classmates.

1. Look at the title of this unit. *Anthropos* is the Greek word for "man." What is anthropology?

2. Look at the title of this chapter. What different types of anthropologists do you think there are?

3. Do you think anthropology can tell us more about the past, the present, or the future? Explain.

Anthropologist Dr. Lee Berger at an excavation site in Gladysvale, South Africa

VOCABULARY PREVIEW

CD 1, TR 1

A Read through the sentences below, which are missing vocabulary from the lecture. Listen to the sentences and write the missing words in the blanks.

1. As Paul Bohannan, _____ anthropologist, pointed out a number of years ago, "Each science that deals with people has its own definitions of *human*."

2. Anthropology attempts to be _____—the study of human behavior in all places and throughout time.

3. Mostly the work of anthropologists is not _____ and involves repetitive and _____ activities.

4. In the modern day, anthropology is a _____ social science with two broad fields and several _____ or subfields.

5. _____ is the study of different cultures through material _____ rather than direct interviews or observations of the group under study.

6. _____, as you probably know, is the study of language as communication among humans.

7. Culture is learned and _____ primarily through language.

8. _____ is the _____ description of human societies, mostly based on firsthand fieldwork.

9. It is important to note that there are several _____ common among all societies.

10. So, you might ask, what are the practical _____ for such a broad field?

B Check the spelling of the vocabulary words with your teacher. Discuss the meanings of these words and any other unfamiliar words in the sentences.

PREDICTIONS

Think about the questions in the Topic Preview on page 2 and the sentences you heard in the Vocabulary Preview. Write three questions that you think will be answered in the lecture. Share your questions with your classmates.

NOTETAKING PREPARATION

Recording Important Information

Efficient notetakers do not write down every word of a lecture. Here are some tips for taking notes:

- Listen for and note the main ideas of the lecture.
- Write only the key words, not complete sentences.
- Use abbreviations for common words or for a specific word that you hear many times in the lecture. There are many ways to abbreviate. Figure out what abbreviations make sense to you. Here are some examples:

  shorten long words to one or two syllables
  problem = *prob*   anthropology = *anthro*

  leave out the vowels
  problem = *prb* or *prblm*

  use a single letter for a high-frequency word
  Egypt = *E*   price = *p*

- When you miss something in the lecture, leave some space.
- After a lecture, go back and write out any words you abbreviated and might not remember later. Check with the lecturer or another student to fill in information you missed.

A Look at the abbreviations. Match the abbreviations to words from the lecture.

1. *devt* _____ cultural
2. *comp* _____ anatomy
3. *anat* _____ development
4. *cult* _____ subjects
5. *subj* _____ comparative

6. *anthro* _____ evolution
7. *phys* _____ analysis
8. *As* _____ physical
9. *evol* _____ anthropologists
10. *anlys* _____ anthropology

🔊 CD 1, TR 2 **B** Listen to sentences from the lecture. Take notes. Use abbreviations where possible.

1. _____
2. _____
3. _____
4. _____
5. _____

◀) FIRST LISTENING
CD 1, TR 3

Listen to the lecture and number the slides on this page and the next in the order they would be shown during the lecture. Write the number of the slide on the line provided and answer the question to the right of the slide.

Subfields of Cultural Anthropology

Archaeology

Linguistics

Ethnography

Psychological anthropology

Slide #_____

What is ethnography?

Universals in All Societies

Anthropology today

• Applied anthropology

Slide #_____

Are anthropologists only interested in the past?

Physical Anthropology

Definition

Related subjects

Ways to study evolution of humans

Slide #_____

What is *physical anthropology?*

What Is Anthropology?

Literal definition

Misconceptions

My definition

Development of anthropology

Slide #_____

What is the lecture going to explain?

Cultural Anthropology

Definition

Study of specific locations or groups
- Margaret Mead
- Clyde Kluckhohn

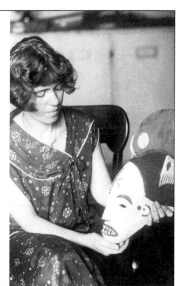

Slide #_____

What is *cultural anthropology?*

🔊 SECOND LISTENING

CD 1, TR 4

Now that you've listened to the lecture once, listen to it again and take notes. Write on a separate piece of paper.

🔊 THIRD LISTENING

CD 1, TR 5

You will hear parts of the lecture again. Look through your notes as you listen. A notetaking mentor will discuss the notes. Circle the answer that is closest to the notes you took, and put a check (✓) next to the notes that the mentor wrote.

Part 1

1. a.

cult anthro = lrnd behav in hum soc

   b.

cultural anthropology = study learned behavior human societies

2. a.

geog areas
- Mead = Samoa
- SW US

   b.

geog areas
- Mead = Samoa
- (Cluckho ??) = SW US

   c.

geog areas
- Mead = Samoa
- Kluckhohn = SW US

Part 2

3. a.

cult anthro — arch — ling — ethno

   b.

cult anthro & sci study hum cult disc in next lecture

   c.

cult anthro subfields:
- arch, ling, ethno

Part 3

4. a.

arch = diff cult — not int, obs

    ex — King Tut 1922

   b.

arch = study of diff'ent cults thru <u>mat srces</u>

   ≠ int'vws + obs'ns
- ex: Tut's tomb 1922

   c.

archaeol'gy is the stud of diff cult's through material sources rather than dir interviews or obs of the grp under study

1 ex — famous arch site disc past cent was K Tut's tomb near (??) Egypt in 1922

CD 1, TR 6

ACCURACY CHECK

You will hear questions about the lecture. Answer each question by referring to the notes that you took while listening to the lecture.

1. a. man
   b. the study of man
   c. a choice-making animal

2. a. history
   b. describing societies
   c. the ideal society

3. a. the Navajo
   b. the Americas
   c. Samoa and New Guinea

4. a. cultural anthropology
   b. physical anthropology
   c. psychological anthropology

5. a. *Mirror for Man*
   b. study of Navajo Indians
   c. research in Samoa and New Guinea

6. a. sociology
   b. ethnology
   c. archaeology

7. a. a universal
   b. skills and attitudes
   c. practical applications of anthropology

8. a. teaching
   b. urban planning
   c. museum administration

ORAL SUMMARY

Use your notes to create an oral summary of the lecture with a partner. As you work together, add details to your notes that your partner included but you had missed.

DISCUSSION

Discuss the following questions with a classmate or in a small group.

1. Anthropology is a very broad field. Where does anthropology end and other fields begin? In other words, what is the difference between anthropology and fields such as history or religion?

2. What was the principal role of the anthropologist in the past and how is that role changing?

3. Can you think of ways that applied anthropology is useful in your community?

PRE-READING

The following Reading is about an anthropologist's findings. Before you read, answer the following questions. Share your answers with a classmate.

1. Look at the title and headings in the Reading article. Write the name of a subfield of anthropology you expect to learn more about in the article.

2. Using information you learned in the lecture, what are two things you expect to learn about the Vikings from an anthropological study?

READING

Now read the article.

Vikings Filed Their Teeth, Skeleton Study Shows

Contrary to popular belief, the Vikings took great pride in their looks. One beautification technique of the ancient Norsemen was to file their teeth. A Swedish anthropologist analyzed 557 Viking skeletons dating from AD 800 to 1050 and discovered that 24 of them bore deep, horizontal grooves across their upper front teeth. It's the first time that dental modification—a practice found in cultures around the world—has been seen in human skeletons from Europe.

"These unique finds of deliberate dental modification . . . reveal what we did not know before, that this custom is practiced around the world and also in Europe," said Caroline Arcini, an anthropologist at the National Heritage Board in Lund, Sweden.

Acquisitive Habits

Researchers say the Vikings may have learned the practice of filing their teeth from a foreign culture. "Vikings are well known for their acquisitive habits, but until now we've thought of this in terms of gold, silver, and booty, not facial decoration," said William Fitzhugh, a Viking expert at the Smithsonian National Museum of Natural History in Washington, D.C.

"Maybe they adopted the idea of mutilating their teeth from people they met on their voyages," Arcini said. "The only place I know of [where people] have similar horizontal filing marks on their teeth . . . is the area of the Great Lakes in North America and the present states of Illinois, Arizona, and Georgia."

Social Identification

People in many cultures have been modifying their teeth for several thousand years. Some of the oldest cases of tooth modification come from Mexico, dating as far back as 1400 BCE. But the Viking discovery is the first historical example of ceremonial dental modification among Europeans.

The skeletons Arcini analyzed were discovered at several Viking-era burial sites in Sweden and

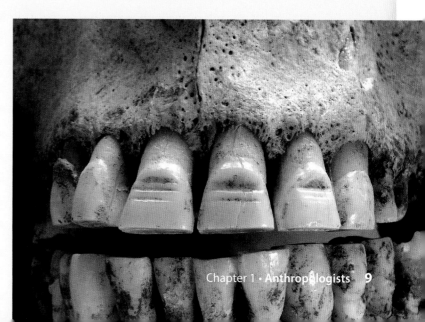

Replica of a Viking wooden church

Denmark. The 24 skeletons she found with filed teeth all belonged to men. The marks were cut deep into the enamel and occurred often in pairs or triplets. "I can conclude that the filed furrows in the front teeth of 24 Viking men are deliberately made and not the result of using the teeth as a tool," Arcini said. She also noted that the marks are so well made that a person of great skill most likely filed them.

Why the Viking men had their teeth modified remains a mystery, but it's likely that the marks represented some kind of achievement. "I think the Vikings' filed furrows should be seen as a social identification," Arcini, the Swedish anthropologist, said. "Maybe they were brave warriors who got a furrow each time they won a battle, or tradesmen who traveled together."

Fitzhugh, of the Smithsonian, says the reasons may have been partly aesthetic. "We do know that the Vikings took pride in their appearance, combed their hair, and ironed their clothes with hot rocks," Fitzhugh said. "They now seem to have taken pain to decorate their teeth."

DISCUSSION

Discuss these questions with a classmate.

1. What surprised or interested you most about the findings described in the passage? Why?

2. How was the information in the reading similar to or different from the information in the lecture?

3. Summarize what you have learned about anthropology and what it can tell us about a people.

RESEARCH PROJECT

Individually or with a partner, find a current article on a discovery that changes how anthropologists think about a people or place. Write up the details for a short presentation to the class.

Be sure to include the following:

• What is the source of your information?

• Under which branch of anthropology does the discovery fall?

• Who sponsored the research or expedition resulting in the finding?

• What are the significant details (who? what? where?) of the finding?

CHAPTER 2

The Concept of Culture

Understanding One Another

TOPIC PREVIEW

Answer the following questions with a partner or your classmates.

1. Look at the title of this chapter. What do we mean by a "concept of culture"? Do you think people have different concepts, or ideas, about what "culture" is?

2. Look at the photograph on this page. What elements of culture does it illustrate?

3. How curious are you about other cultures? Do you know students from other cultures? In what ways, if any, do you seem different?

Ethnic Papua New Guinean in traditional dress at a sing-sing festival

VOCABULARY PREVIEW

CD 1, TR 7

A Read through the sentences below, which are missing vocabulary from the lecture. Listen to the sentences and write the missing words in the blanks.

1. Culture is that _____ whole which includes knowledge, belief, art, law, morals, custom, and any other capabilities and habits _____ by man as a member of society.

2. Another definition of culture that many find useful is "the totality of learned, socially _____ behavior."

3. Ned Seelye, in his 1993 book *Teaching Culture*, lists six skills to _____ and support _____ communication.

4. _____ curiosity about another culture and _____ toward its members.

5. Recognize that different roles and other social _____ such as age, sex, social class, religion, _____, and place of residence affect the way people speak and behave.

6. Realize that effective communication requires discovering the culturally _____ images of people when they think, act, and react to the world around them.

7. Recognize that _____ variables and _____ shape people's behavior in important ways.

8. Understand that people generally act the way they do because they are _____ the options their society allows for _____ basic physical and psychological needs.

9. Culture and society must _____.

10. In the long history of human life, _____ is a fairly recent _____.

B Check the spelling of the vocabulary words with your teacher. Discuss the meanings of these words and any other unfamiliar words in the sentences.

PREDICTIONS

Think about the questions in the Topic Preview on page 11 and the sentences you heard in the Vocabulary Preview. Write three questions that you think will be answered in the lecture. Share your questions with your classmates.

NOTETAKING PREPARATION

Recording Information as a List

Listen for cues that show a lecturer is going to list information. Use a heading and numbers, letters, or bullets to show the information clearly. Here are some examples.

Cues to listen for	Notes

The report gave two reasons for the failure
    First, . . .
    Then, . . .
	Why fail —
	1.
	2.

Let me give you some examples of this type of problem
    One is . . .
    Another . . .
    The last . . .
    Finally, . . .
	Ex of prob
	•
	
	•
	
	•
	
	•

A **Look at the notes below and answer the questions.**

1. Who do you think Benedict, Tylor, and Morgan are?

2. What do you think the following abbreviations stand for?
   a. hum'ty   b. stgs   c. civiliz   d. for. lang

3. How many answers are given to the question at the beginning of the notes?

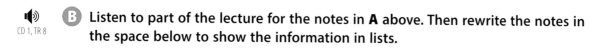

Why stdy cult anthro? Benedict says stry hum'ty fasc (Tylor & Morgan – cult devt = 3 stgs – savg'ry, barb'ism, civiliz) lrn & use for. lang

B **Listen to part of the lecture for the notes in A above. Then rewrite the notes in the space below to show the information in lists.**

CD 1, TR 8

◀》 FIRST LISTENING
CD 1, TR 9

Listen to the lecture and number the slides on this page and the next in the order they would be shown during the lecture. Write the number of the slide on the line provided and answer the question to the right of the slide.

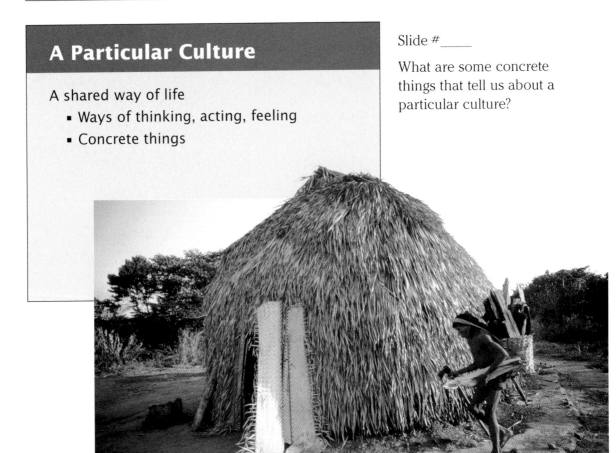

Coexistence of Culture and Society

Isolated cultures

Multicultural or pluralist

Subcultures

Slide #_____

What is an example of a pluralist society?

A Particular Culture

A shared way of life
- Ways of thinking, acting, feeling
- Concrete things

Slide #_____

What are some concrete things that tell us about a particular culture?

Similarities Across Cultures

Importance of discovering similarities

Universals among societies

The role of the individual

Slide #_____

How many "universals" among all cultures does the lecturer mention?

Cultural Anthropology

Why study cultural anthropology?
- Fascinating story of cultural growth
- Learn and use a foreign language
- Intercultural understanding

Slide #_____

What is the definition of cultural anthropology?

What Is Culture?

Murdock / Tylor / Kessing

Learned, socially transmitted behavior

Slide #_____

How many categories did Murdock list?

SECOND LISTENING

Now that you've listened to the lecture once, listen to it again and take notes. Write on a separate piece of paper.

THIRD LISTENING

You will hear parts of the lecture again. Look through your notes as you listen. A notetaking mentor will discuss the notes. Circle the answer that is closest to the notes you took, and put a check (✓) next to the notes that the mentor wrote.

Part 1

1. a.

Cult anthro = study of cult, liv & dead. In total includes ling, arch, ethnology

b.

Cult anthro = st. of cult (liv & dead)
- ling = study spch frms
- arch = " dead cult
- ethno = " liv cult (can be obs)

Part 2

2. a.

Teaching Culture – 6 skills
1. cult curiosty
2. rec roles aff spk & beh
3. rlize eff comm req disc cult-cond'd imgs
4. rec sit'l var shap beh
5. und. ppl act bec ex opt'ns to sat phys & psych nds
6. dev ablty to eval gen'ztion & loc/org info

b.

Sealy (sp??) – skills for intc'l comm
1. curiosty & emp
2. rec roles aff spk & beh
3. rlize eff comm req disc cult-cond'd imgs
4. rec sit'l var shap beh
5. und ppl act bec ex opt'ns to sat phys & psych nds
6. dev ablty to eval gen'ztion & loc/org info

c.

1. curiosty & emp
2. rec roles aff spk & beh
3. rlize eff comm req disc cult-cond'd imgs
4. rec sit'l var shap beh
5. und. ppl act bec ex opt'ns to sat phys & psych nds
6. dev ablty to eval gen'ztion & loc/org info

Part 3

3. a.

Universals
1. rewards & punishment
2. withhld info fr young
3. contr cult educ yng

b.

Universals of culture – rewds & punshmt – wthhld info – incl faults in ldrs – taboos – educ young for dom pos

c.

Univs'ls
- use rwds & pnish't to enc corr beh.
- wihld info (eg ldrs, taboos)
- ctrl'g cult educ yng to strngthn dom pos

ACCURACY CHECK

CD 1, TR 12

You will hear questions about the lecture. Answer each question by referring to the notes that you took while listening to the lecture.

1. a. Mead
    b. Tylor
    c. Murdock

2. a. savagery
    b. language
    c. barbarism

3. a. 1962
    b. 1989
    c. 1993

4. a. communication
    b. social variables
    c. empathy and curiosity

5. a. a remote tribe
    b. a pluralistic society
    c. people in a large city

6. a. civilization
    b. savagery
    c. multiculturalism

7. a. political
    b. military
    c. informal

8. a. Seelye
    b. Sapir
    c. Benedict

ORAL SUMMARY

Use your notes to create an oral summary of the lecture with a partner. As you work together, add details to your notes that your partner included but you had missed.

DISCUSSION

Discuss the following questions with a classmate or in a small group.

1. After listening to the lecture, do you find *culture* difficult or easy to define? What is your definition? In what ways is it the same or different from definitions in the lecture?

2. List four or five cultural "generalizations" that foreigners may have about your country.

3. "If a group or society is small, isolated, and stable, it might also share a single culture." Do you know of any such "single" cultures in the world? What would you look for to decide if a group of people share a "single" culture?

PRE-READING

The following Reading is about the experiences of an anthropological research team in the mountains of Papua New Guinea. Before you read, answer the following questions. Share your answers with a classmate.

1. Look at the title of the article and the photograph on the next page. Write two things that you expect to learn about the "Cave People" from the article.

2. In the lecture, the speaker discussed reasons to study cultural anthropology. Why would a team of researchers want to visit these people in Papua New Guinea?

READING

Now read the article.

Last of the Cave People

The vast geographic variation of Papua New Guinea created tremendous biological diversity, which in turn was accompanied by enormous cultural diversity. It is only in the most deeply inaccessible regions that enclaves of traditionally nomadic people, like the Meakambut, still exist. The Meakambut were unknown to the outside world until the 1960s. In 1991 anthropologist Borut Telban spent a week in the area and found only 11 Meakambut. When Telban returned in 2001, he couldn't locate them again.

In hopes of meeting up with these last semi-nomadic holdouts, an anthropological researcher named Nancy Sullivan sent out a team to find the Meakambut and inventory their caves. Sullivan's team discovered 52 surviving Meakambut and 105 caves with names.

Our team flies into the Sepik River basin. We skim up smaller and smaller tributaries in a motor dugout. Finally we strike out on foot into the mountains. We try reaching the Meakambut by jungle telephone: Three men pound the trunk of a towering tree with wooden bats. When this doesn't work, we set out on a two-day trek to the group's last known whereabouts.

At noon the next day, two Meakambut men come striding into our camp. They recognize Joshua Meraveka, a member of Sullivan's team. He introduces them as John and Mark Aiyo. John is a leader of the Meakambut. While waiting there for the rest of the Embarakal to arrive, John explains cave life to me. He says they like their hunter-gatherer life and have no interest in changing it.

Before long, the rest of the Meakambut arrive. This is when we first encounter Lidia, curled up by the fire, coughing horribly. A member of our team, an emergency medical technician, examines Lidia. He determines that she likely has a life-threatening case of pneumonia and gives her double doses of antibiotics and Tylenol. We suggest that first thing in the morning she be carried out of the mountains, to a clinic in the village of Amboin. Two other Meakambut are also seriously ill.

One man from our team, Sebastian Haraha, is an ethnographer who has come to pinpoint the locations of the Meakambut's caves. He hopes to register them so the homeland of the Meakambut will be protected. Now, he volunteers to escort the sick.

Two nights later, John begins to let down his guard. He admits that his group hasn't eaten meat or killed a pig for over three months. He is deeply worried for his people. When the campfire dies out, John whispers something he wants me to pass on to the government of Papua New Guinea.

The next morning our team leaves the mountains. We reach our motor dugout and travel downstream

A member of the Meakambut tribe wearing bird-feather headdress

completely gone, and their culture and language would vanish. When I get back to Port Moresby, I'm going to walk straight into the prime minister's office and do something."

I nod and pass along John's message: "We, the Meakambut people, will give up hunting and always moving and living in the mountain caves if the government will give us a health clinic and a school, and two shovels and two axes, so we can build homes."

to the village of Awim and learn that Lidia and the others are here. Lidia is alive. Simple antibiotics have saved her.

At breakfast, I find Sebastian Haraha. "Protecting the caves? What does it matter if there are no Meakambut left?" asks Sebastian. "The Meakambut are on the edge of extinction. They are dying from easily treatable illnesses. In ten years they could be

The Meakambut continue to live without access to government services. But they have partly settled in homes on the ridgetop camp of Tembakapa. Despite the threat of encroachment by miners, they continue to hunt and gather on their traditional land.

DISCUSSION

Discuss these questions with a classmate.

1. What surprised or interested you most about the culture described in the passage? Why?

2. What was the role of the anthropologists in this story? How was it similar to or different from what you learned about anthropologists and ethnologists in the lecture?

3. What information from the lecture was exemplified in the article?

RESEARCH PROJECT

Individually or in a group, research one of the following topics. Write a short paper on the topic, or plan and present a group presentation to inform the class about the topic.

1. Isolated cultures: Where do they still exist, and what challenges do they face?

2. Research in cultural anthropology: What similarities and differences exist between your culture and another?

3. Intercultural understanding: Does studying or living in another culture change an individual's values? Provide evidence to support your opinion.

4. Another related topic that interests you or your group.

BEFORE VIEWING

TOPIC PREVIEW

What do you think it would be like to be a professional photographer who travels around the world? Write some pros and cons of the job. Discuss your answers with a partner.

Pros	Cons

VOCABULARY PREVIEW

A Read the definitions of these key words and phrases that you will hear during the video.

hanging out with spending leisure time with

flexibility the ability to easily adjust to new situations

had language in common shared the same language

set up camp find a new place to start a home and live

on assignment carrying out a job you are hired to do as a journalist or photographer

compelling so interesting that you want to pay close attention to it

immerse yourself become completely involved in something

abide by follow a particular law, custom, rule, etc.

inspirational making you feel excited and have creative ideas

B **Work with a partner and write in the blank the word from the box that best completes the sentence.**

communities	culture	kids	photographers
spend	stories	travelers	unusual

1. Annie's children travel with her to foreign countries and _____ a lot of time **hanging out with** _____ from other cultures.

2. When making friends in new _____, people don't always **have** the same **language in common**.

3. **Flexibility** is an important quality for professional _____ **on assignment** because they might have to **set up camp** in some _____ places.

4. Experienced _____ know that it is important to **abide by** the customs of the culture you are visiting.

5. You can **immerse yourself** in another _____, even if you can't speak the language.

6. When photographs are **compelling** and **inspirational**, it makes people want to read the _____ that accompany them.

VIEWING

🖥 FIRST VIEWING

Watch the video, and then compare your first impressions with a partner. Talk about what you remember, what surprised you, and what interested you.

🖥 SECOND VIEWING

Watch the video again. Listen for the missing words and write them in the blanks.

1. Our kids have traveled to every continent except _____. More importantly, when we travel they have lived in communities. We never stayed in _____.

2. If you go into each culture open, and look people in the _____ and observe and listen, you're going to make connections that are well beyond what most _____ get to see.

3. And so the real challenge for a photographer is to bring her or his own unique _____ to that subject _____.

4. The camera has always given me an _____ to walk up to people and spend time with them and even go _____ with them.

Complete these notes as you watch the video. Write only important words, not full sentences, and abbreviate common words.

1. Our kids
   - trav ev cont – _____
   - _____
   - not always lang in comm but always fun
   - confident
   - daught 18, no probs trav
   - understand all ppl _____
   - v flexible _____

2. Challenge of photog
   - bring a unique _____
   - tell a _____
   - compel ppl to _____

3. Lessons learned in trav
   - allow self to immers → _____
   - _____ gd lang skills
   - be a guest, i.e., follow _____

ORAL SUMMARY

Use your notes to create an oral summary of the video with your partner. As you work together, add details to your notes that your partner included but you had missed.

DISCUSSION

Discuss the following questions with a classmate or in a small group.

1. Think about what you learned in this unit. In what ways is a photographer a type of anthropologist?

2. What is Annie Griffiths' advice for communicating with people from different cultures? Do you agree with her? Why or why not?

3. Why does Annie Griffiths say regular travel is spoiled for her?

4. After listening to Annie Griffiths, would you like to be a travel photographer? Why or why not?

History
The Passing of Time and Civilizations

Detail of a mural tomb painting of Thutmose III, Luxor Museum, Luxor, Egypt

3

The Egyptian Pyramids

Houses of Eternity

TOPIC PREVIEW

Answer the following questions with a partner or your classmates.

1. What do you know about the pyramids of Egypt? Who built them? When?

2. Look at the title of this chapter. Why is a pyramid called a *house of eternity*?

3. Grave robbers are people who steal things from burial places. Why were grave robbers very interested in the pyramids?

Stone building blocks of the Great Pyramid

Pyramids at Giza, near Cairo, Egypt

VOCABULARY PREVIEW

CD 1, TR 13

A **Read through the sentences below, which are missing vocabulary from the lecture. Listen to the sentences and write the missing words in the blanks.**

1. To many people throughout the world, some of the most remarkable and puzzling _____ of ancient times are the pyramids of ancient Egypt.

2. Even though many of the pyramids are in _____, they still give us some idea of the magnificence of ancient Egypt's _____.

3. Remember, when we're talking about ancient Egypt, we're talking about at least 30 _____ dynasties.

4. So when a person died, and especially when a _____ died, in order to ensure his eternal life, he had his body embalmed or _____.

5. In other words, he had his _____ dried out and wrapped in linen to _____ it from decay.

6. You see, the ancient Egyptians really believed that if one's mummy was destroyed, then his or her _____ would be destroyed.

7. For another thing, the ancient Egyptians believed that the dead person could take his or her earthly _____ along to the next world.

8. Anyway, the dead person was provided with food, clothing, furniture, _____, and even servants.

9. It seems that local builders and conquerors found it convenient to _____ off the limestone from the pyramids and use it to build with.

10. And yet, what is so _____ is that even these _____ did not escape the attacks of the grave robbers.

B **Check the spelling of the vocabulary words with your teacher. Discuss the meanings of these words and any other unfamiliar words in the sentences.**

PREDICTIONS

Think about the questions in the Topic Preview on page 24 and the sentences you heard in the Vocabulary Preview. Write three questions that you think will be answered in the lecture. Share your questions with your classmates.

NOTETAKING PREPARATION

Recording Numbers and Dates in Notes

Lectures often include numbers and dates. There are many different ways that numbers are stated. Here are some examples:

2010   **twenty ten** or **two thousand and ten** (listen for the reduced *n* instead of *and*)

2,500,000   **two and a half billion** or **2.5 billion** ("2 point 5 billion")

When taking notes about numbers, the following are useful abbreviations:

2000→	since 2000	K	thousand	ht	height
←2000	until 2000	M	million	wt	weight
950–2000	from 950 to 2000	B	billion	'	foot, feet
C20	20th century	m	meter(s)	"	inch, inches
bce	before the common era	km	kilometer(s)	~	about, approximately
↓	lower, decrease, less	g	gram(s)	=	is, are, have, equals
↑	higher, increase, more	kg	kilogram(s)	≤	at least

A Look at the notes. What do they mean?

1. 2614–2502 bce _____

2. ~2.3 M _____

3. ~15K kg _____

4. ht=147m _____

5. 3 m ↓ _____

6. 2500 kg _____

🔊 CD 1, TR 14

B Listen to sentences from the lecture. Take notes. Use symbols and abbreviations where possible.

1. _____

2. _____

3. _____

4. _____

5. _____

6. _____

FIRST LISTENING
CD 1, TR 15

Listen to the lecture and number the slides on this page and the next in the order they would be shown during the lecture. Write the number of the slide on the line provided and answer the question to the right of the slide.

Lesser Pyramids

Later Dynasties
1786 BCE

Slide #_____

What is the area called where these tombs were found?

Evolution of Pyramids

Third Dynasty
2664–2615 BCE

Slide #_____

What is the name of this type of pyramid?

Great Pyramids

Fourth Dynasty
2614–2502 BCE

Slide #_____

Where are these pyramids?

Structure of Pyramids

First and Second Dynasties
3100–2665 BCE

Slide #_____

What is the name of the type of tomb the pharaohs first built?

The Pyramids of Egypt

What do the ruins of the pyramids show us about ancient Egyptian civilization?
- Belief in the afterlife
- Grave robbers common

Slide #_____

Why were the pyramids built?

🔊 SECOND LISTENING
CD 1, TR 16

Now that you've listened to the lecture once, listen to it again and take notes. Write on a separate piece of paper.

🔊 THIRD LISTENING
CD 1, TR 17

You will hear parts of the lecture again. Look through your notes as you listen. A notetaking mentor will discuss the notes. Circle the answer that is closest to the notes you took, and put a check (✓) next to the notes that the mentor wrote.

Part 1

1. a. Egypt   b. Eg.   c. E.   d. Egy

2. a. the pyramids   b. pyds   c. P's   d. pyr's

3. a. 3,000 yrs.   b. 300 years   c. 3K yrs   d. three thousand years

4. a. dyn. = series K's & Q's   b. dyn.: Romanovs, Ming, Al-Saud

Part 2

5. a. bench   b. shoebox   c. low, flat   d. rect.

Part 3

6. a.

<u>"typical" pyr</u>
- 3rd Dyn – 2664–2614
- King ~~So~~ Zoser
- arch. = Imhotep
- "step" pyr = pile mastabas

b.

Next style – typical
- 3rd dyn
- Zoser, Imhotep

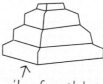

↑
pile of mastabas

c.

B. the "typical" pyramid was built in Third Dynasty (2664–2615 BCE)

1. Built for King ZOSER by architect [IMH   ]???
2. pile of mastabas

ACCURACY CHECK

CD 1, TR 18

You will hear questions about the lecture. Answer each question by referring to the notes that you took while listening to the lecture.

1. a. 20
    b. 30
    c. 40

2. a. to remember the pharaohs
    b. to send the pharoahs into the afterlife
    c. to show people the wealth of the pharaohs

3. a. servants
    b. clothing
    c. a pyramid

4. a. underground
    b. mastaba
    c. step

5. a. near Cairo
    b. in Alexandria
    c. Luxor

6. a. Khufu
    b. Cheops
    c. King

7. a. 2.3 million
    b. 2,500
    c. 15,000

8. a. It was a step pyramid.
    b. It was underground.
    c. It was in Giza.

ORAL SUMMARY

Use your notes to create an oral summary of the lecture with a partner. As you work together, add details to your notes that your partner had included but which you had missed.

DISCUSSION

Discuss the following questions with a classmate or in a small group.

1. The construction of pyramids was an example of the search for everlasting life. In what other ways have people searched for immortality?

2. Why did King Thutmose I decide not to be buried in a pyramid? In what other ways do you think the Egyptian pharaohs could have solved the problems they encountered with their system of burial?

3. What do you think is the most interesting structure in the world? The Eiffel Tower? The Great Wall of China? A structure in your country? List three reasons why you find this structure interesting and share these reasons with a partner.

PRE-READING

The following Reading is about the Egyptian pharaoh Ramses II. Before you read, answer the following questions. Share your answers with a classmate.

1. Using the information about pharaohs from the lecture, write three statements you expect to be true about Ramses II.

2. In the lecture, the speaker mentioned that the pharaohs were mummified. What do you remember about this technique for preserving bodies? If you could learn three more things about mummification, what would you want to find out?

READING

Now read the article.

Ramses the Great

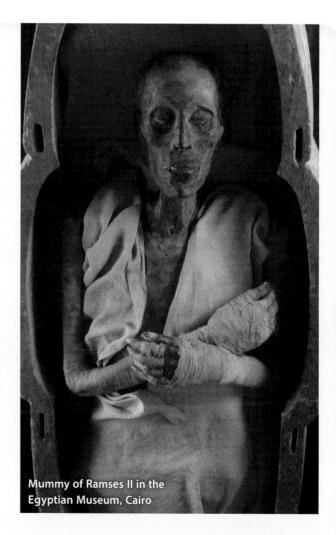

Mummy of Ramses II in the Egyptian Museum, Cairo

On my last day in Egypt I finally receive permission from the Egyptian Antiquities Organization to see Ramses' mummy. My colleague, Lou Mazzatenta, is also permitted to photograph the pharaoh. At the Egyptian Museum in Cairo, conservation director Nasry Iskander lifts the dark velvet off the mummy case. I behold the face. Browned and chisel sharp. Arms crossed regally across the chest. A long neck, a proud aquiline nose, and wisps of reddish hair, probably colored by his embalmers.

Ramses' mummification and burial rites likely took the traditional 70 days. Embalmers removed internal organs, placing the liver, lungs, stomach, and intestines in sacred jars. His heart was sealed in his body. Egyptians believed that it was the source of intellect as well as feeling and would be required for the final judgment. Only if a heart was as light as the feather of truth would the god Osiris receive its owner into the afterlife.

Egyptians did not appreciate the brain. The embalmers drew it out through the nose and threw it away.

After they dried the corpse with natron salt, the embalmers washed the body and coated it with preserving resins. Finally they wrapped it in hundreds of yards of linen.

Within 150 years of Ramses' burial, his tomb was robbed by thieves and his mummy desecrated. Twice reburied by priests, the body retained some of its secrets. X-ray examination of the body indicated that Ramses suffered badly from arthritis in the hip, which would have forced him to stoop. His teeth were severely worn, and he had dental abscesses and gum disease.

The photography finished, the velvet is replaced over Ramses' mummy—but the face stays with me. Not the face of Shelley's Ozymandias, not that of a god, but the face of a man. Was Ramses bombastic, cruel, ego driven? By our standards, certainly. He left no evidence of the human complexity or the bitterly learned insights that redeem such proudful mythic kings as Oedipus, or Shakespeare's King Lear, but he did love deeply and lose. And all those children who died before him—Ramses knew human suffering. Did he really believe he was a god? Who can say? But clearly, he strove to be the king his country expected—providing wealth and security—and succeeded. More than most, this man got what he wanted.

Sarcophagus containing the mummy of Pharaoh Ramses II

DISCUSSION

Discuss these questions with a classmate.

1. What surprised or interested you most about the mummification process described in the passage? Why?

2. How was the information in the reading similar to or different from the information in the lecture?

3. Summarize what you have learned about beliefs of ancient Egyptians from both the lecture and the article.

RESEARCH PROJECT

Individually or in a group, research one of the following topics. Write a short paper on the topic or plan and present a group presentation to inform the class about the topic.

1. The discovery of the tomb of the boy pharaoh, King Tutankhamen

2. The pyramid of Cheops

3. The pyramids of Mayan and Aztec culture in South America

4. The life of Ramses II or another ancient Egyptian king or queen

5. Another question that interests you or your group

CHAPTER 4

The First Emperor of China

Building an Empire and a House of Eternity

TOPIC PREVIEW

Answer the following questions with a partner or your classmates.

1. Look at the title of this chapter. The first emperor of China was named Qin Shi Huang. How does a leader of a country build an empire?

2. Look at the photo. Why do you think the emperor had statues of soldiers in his tomb?

3. What are some differences you can see between this "House of Eternity" and the Pyramids?

Terra-cotta warriors from the tomb complex of Qin Shi Huang

VOCABULARY PREVIEW

🔊
CD 2, TR 1

A Read through the sentences below, which are missing vocabulary from the lecture. Listen to the sentences and write the missing words in the blanks.

1. _____ find out about these ancient times by studying the ruins of cities, monuments, or tombs, or any written records that remain.

2. The history part of my talk will be about Qin Shi Huang, who was the _____ of the first unified empire in China.

3. Today, I'm also going to be talking about what has been found, to _____, in the area of Qin Shi Huang's tomb.

4. Before Qin Shi Huang unified the empire in 221 BCE, China had been torn apart by wars between seven regional _____.

5. When Qin Shi Huang became Emperor, he decreed that a _____ system of Chinese _____ was to be used throughout the empire.

6. In the second year after unification, _____ of three major _____ highways was begun.

7. At this point, I'm going to _____ from talking about the _____ of Qin Shi Huang to the archaeology part of my lecture.

8. It seems that as soon as the Emperor gained power, he became _____ with death, and with constructing a magnificent House of Eternity for his afterlife.

9. The entire area of the tomb covers _____ 56.25 square kilometers.

10. It is even believed that _____ was pumped through the tomb to create the image of flowing rivers in the tomb area.

11. Without a doubt, the most striking _____ of the Emperor Qin's House of Eternity are the _____ warriors and horses found in the tomb area.

12. Chinese officials say that the tomb mound of the first Chinese emperor will not be _____ until preservation techniques have advanced significantly.

B Check the spelling of the vocabulary words with your teacher. Discuss the meanings of these words and any other unfamiliar words in the sentences.

PREDICTIONS

Think about the questions in the Topic Preview on page 33 and the sentences you heard in the Vocabulary Preview. Write three questions that you think will be answered in the lecture. Share your questions with your classmates.

NOTETAKING PREPARATION

Using Indentation and Spacing Effectively in Notes

When you take notes, your use of space on the page can help you review your notes. Here are some tips:

- Align information that has the same level of importance. For example, begin main ideas on the left margin of your paper. Indent supporting information.
- Leave extra space on one side to add more information or notes later.
- Skip one line between ideas. Skip several lines to show a new topic.
- Don't worry about trying to make a formal outline of a lecture. Very few lecturers follow an outline.

A **Look at the notes below and answer the questions.**

1. Identify the main idea.

2. Identify two specific points.

3. Why is there space in the middle of the last line and question marks at the end? Where do you think the notetaker can find out the missing information?

Q.S, unif. emp. 221 bce – def. 6 K'doms
    1. end pwr 6 K'doms
    2. centr. imp. syst., → > [   ] yrs   ???

CD 2, TR 2

B **Listen to the part of the lecture for the notes in A above. Fill in the missing information. Then rewrite the notes below in the space provided so the notes show main ideas and specific facts more effectively.**

QS unif. & prot. emp. 1st, stand'ize
syst char. 2nd 1 syst. wts. & meas., 1 syst. curr.

FIRST LISTENING

CD 2, TR 3

Listen to the lecture and number the slides on this page and the next in the order they would be shown during the lecture. Write the number of the slide on the line provided and answer the question to the right of the slide.

Unification

Standardization of systems in the empire

Protection of the empire
  ▪ Ordered building of Great Wall

Slide #_____

What was the first thing that Qin Shi Huang standardized?

Construction of Tomb

Replica of Qin capital

Terra-cotta warriors and horses

Slide #_____

What was used to resemble a flowing river?

First Emperor of China
Building an Empire and a House of Eternity

History ⟷ Archaeology

Qin Shi Huang ⟷ Tomb

Slide #____

When was Qin Shi Huang's tomb discovered?

Excavation of Tomb

Museum (1975) covers 3 pits of excavation site

Slide #____

Have archaeologists finished excavating the entire tomb?

Historical Context

China – divided into regional kingdoms
- Ying Zheng – King of Qin

Qin unified China
- Centralized imperial system begins
- Lasts 2,000 years

Slide #____

How many kingdoms did Ying Zheng defeat?

SECOND LISTENING

Now that you've listened to the lecture once, listen to it again and take notes. Write on a separate piece of paper.

THIRD LISTENING

You will hear parts of the lecture again. Look through your notes as you listen. A notetaking mentor will discuss the notes. Circle the answer below which is closest to the notes you took, and put a check (✓) next to the notes that the mentor wrote.

Part 1

1. a.

> to protect empire — Great Wall of China already 3 walls — joined 1500 miles also 3 highways — 6,800 km (4,225 miles)

b.

> to protect E. –
> GWall
> • 3 sm. walls bef.
> • 1500 mi.
> 3 hwys
> • 6800 km

Part 2

2. a.

> 3 maj. hwys
> • 6800 km
> > Rom. E. rds

b.

> 3 hwys
> • 6800 km / 4225 mi
> 150 C.E. Rom E. rds
> • 5,984 km / 3718 mi

Part 3

3. a.

> > Rom. E. rds
> + constr. proj. = tomb
> bio. → arch

b.

> > Rom. E. rds
> tomb/maus.
> preoc. w/ death
> <u>arch.</u>

c.

> > Rom. E. rds
> tomb
>
> Part 2 – (arch.) QS's tomb

CD 2, TR 6

ACCURACY CHECK

You will hear questions about the lecture. Answer each question by referring to the notes that you took while listening to the lecture.

1. a. 210 BCE
   b. 215 BCE
   c. 259 BCE

2. a. 215 BCE
   b. 259 BCE
   c. 221 BCE

3. a. to standardize things
   b. to unify the empire
   c. to protect his empire

4. a. 500 miles
   b. 1,500 miles
   c. 5,000 miles

5. a. 6,800
   b. 68,000
   c. 700,000

6. a. 11 years
   b. 17 years
   c. 70 years

7. a. 56.25 square kilometers
   b. 12,000 square meters
   c. 16,300 square meters

8. a. dead soldiers
   b. ancient rivers
   c. mercury

ORAL SUMMARY

Use your notes to create an oral summary of the lecture with a partner. As you work together, add details to your notes that your partner had included but which you had missed.

DISCUSSION

Discuss the following questions with a classmate or in a small group.

1. Provide examples of the changes Qin Shi Huang made when he became emperor. Why were these changes necessary and important?

2. The lecturer says it is necessary to set the historical context for understanding the archaeological find of Qin Shi Huang's terra-cotta army. Why is knowing the historical context important for modern-day archaeologists and tourists to the site?

3. Explain what is holding up full excavation of the Emperor's tomb. When do archaeologists suspect the tomb may be fully excavated? In the near or distant future? Why?

4. Discuss the ways in which the pharaohs of ancient Egypt and the emperors of ancient China were similar and different in terms of their views of life and death and their preparation for the afterlife.

PRE-READING

The following Reading is about the discovery and excavation of the tomb of Qin Shi Huang. Before you read, answer the following questions. Share your answers with a classmate.

1. Look at the title and headings in the article. Write two ways in which this article will be similar to the lecture and two ways in which it may be different.

2. In the lecture, the speaker only gave the dates when the tomb was discovered. If you could learn two more things about this, what would you want to find out?

READING

Now read the article.

Terra-Cotta Army Protects First Emperor's Tomb

Workers digging a well outside the city of Xi'an, China, in 1974 struck upon one of the greatest archaeological discoveries in the world: a life-size clay soldier poised for battle. The diggers notified Chinese authorities, who dispatched government archaeologists to the site. They found not one, but thousands of clay soldiers, each with unique facial expressions and positioned according to rank. And though largely gray today, patches of paint hint at once brightly colored clothes. Further excavations have revealed swords, arrow tips, and other weapons, many in pristine condition.

The soldiers are in trenchlike, underground corridors. In some of the corridors, clay horses are aligned four abreast; behind them are wooden chariots. The terra-cotta army, as it is known, is part of an elaborate mausoleum created to accompany the first emperor of China into the afterlife, according to archaeologists.

Young Emperor

Ying Zheng took the throne in 246 BC at the age of 13. By 221 BC he had unified a collection of warring kingdoms and taken the name of Qin Shi Huang Di—the First Emperor of Qin. During his rule, Qin standardized coins, weights, and measures; interlinked the states with canals and roads; and is credited for building the first version of the Great Wall.

According to writings of court historian Siam Qian during the following Han dynasty, Qin ordered the mausoleum's construction shortly after taking the throne. More than 700,000 laborers worked on the project, which was halted in 209 BC amid uprisings a year after Qin's death.

To date, four pits have been partially excavated. Three are filled with the terra-cotta soldiers, horse-drawn chariots, and weapons. The fourth pit is empty, a testament to the original unfinished construction. Archaeologists estimate the pits may contain as many as 8,000 figures, but the total may never be known.

Unexcavated Tomb

Qin's tomb itself remains unexcavated, though Siam Qian's writings suggest even greater treasures. "The tomb was filled with models of palaces, pavilions and offices as well as fine vessels, precious stones and rarities," reads a translation of the text. The account indicates the tomb contains replicas of the area's rivers and streams made with mercury flowing to the sea through hills and mountains of bronze. Precious stones such as pearls are said to represent the sun, moon, and other stars.

Modern tests on the tomb mound have revealed unusually high concentrations of mercury, lending credence to at least some of the historical account. Chinese archaeologists are also using remote-sensing technology to probe the tomb mound. The technique recently revealed an underground chamber with four stairlike walls. An archaeologist working on the site told the Chinese press that the chamber may have been built for the soul of the emperor.

Pieces of the terra-cotta army are still being recovered and assembled.

Experimental pits dug around the tomb have revealed dancers, musicians, and acrobats full of life and caught in mid-performance, a sharp contrast to the military poses of the famous terra-cotta soldiers. But further excavations of the tomb itself are on hold, at least for now. "It is best to keep the ancient tomb untouched, because of the complex conditions inside," Duan Qinbao, a researcher with the Shaanxi Provincial Archaeology Institute, told the *China Daily* in 2006.

DISCUSSION

Discuss these questions with a classmate.

1. What surprised or interested you most about the discovery and excavation work described in the passage? Why?

2. How was the information in the article similar to or different from the information in the lecture?

3. Summarize what you have learned about the first emperor of China and his House of Eternity from both the lecture and the article.

RESEARCH PROJECT

Individually or in a group, research one of the following topics. Write a short paper on the topic or plan and present a group presentation to inform the class about the topic.

1. Future excavation of the Emperor's tomb. What is holding it up? Will it ever be fully excavated?

2. The archaeological process of unearthing the tombs and artifacts

3. Another great archaeological discovery

4. Another related topic that interests you or your group

BEFORE VIEWING

TOPIC PREVIEW

Name an ancient site that you have visited or that you know about. Write three facts about this site. Then share your information with a partner.

Site: _____

_____

_____

_____

VOCABULARY PREVIEW

A Read the definitions of these key words that you will hear during the video.

inscriptions writing carved into metal or stone

mason a skilled person who makes or builds things with stone or bricks

slab a thick, flat piece of something such as a large, smooth area of stone

altar a table or other raised, flat surface, used for religious ceremonies

hollow having empty space on the inside; not solid

jacks tools for lifting heavy items such as cars

reconstructed put something together again that was broken apart

aura a feeling that comes from a person, place, or thing

B Work with a partner and write vocabulary from **A** in the blanks in the sentences.

1. We know from the _____ that Pakal, one the greatest of all Maya kings, was born in the year 603 AD.

2. A stone structure with a flat top looked like an _____, but the archaeologists weren't sure what it was.

3. The head _____ suggested drilling a hole in the side of the stone structure to see if it was _____.

4. The archaeologists used 15 automobile _____ to lift up the heavy stone _____.

5. The ancient palace has an incredible _____ about it; everyone who visits is amazed.

VIEWING

🖥 FIRST VIEWING

Watch the video, and then compare your first impressions with a partner. Talk about what you remember, what surprised you, and what interested you.

🖥 SECOND VIEWING

Watch the video again. Listen for the missing words and write them in the blanks.

1. As you can see from this wonderful photograph, the site itself—Palenque—sits on a kind of a _____.

2. The floor of the temple was made out of big, stone slabs with _____ in them. So Alberto had the workers pull up the _____.

3. We went into town and got 15 automobile jacks and pulled the thing up, and there was a _____ inside.

4. His full name was K'inich Janaab' Pakal, and he was the _____ king of Palenque, one of the greatest of all Maya kings.

5. He was covered in jade, as a good Maya king would be. A jade collar, jade bracelets, and an _____ mask as well.

6. Years and years after he's dead, Pakal is still at the _____ of everything.

Jade death mask of King Pakal

⌨ THIRD VIEWING

Complete the time lines as you watch the video. Write your notes next to the dates.

Palenque archaeology

1934

1948 – started

   – summer

1952 – June

Pakal

603 AD

615 AD

Today

ORAL SUMMARY

Use your notes to create an oral summary of the video with a partner. As you work together, add details to your notes that your partner included but you had missed.

DISCUSSION

Discuss the following questions with a classmate or in a small group.

1. What do you know about other ancient burial practices? In what ways was the burial of the Mayan King Pakal similar or different?

2. Who was Juan Chablé? Why was he important to this project?

3. Why does David Stuart say that Palenque is "Pakal City"?

4. After listening to this lecture, do you think you would like to be an archaeologist? Why or why not?

Sociology

The Changing World of Work

Office block at night in
Dusseldorf, Germany

The Distributed Workforce

Where and When People Work

TOPIC PREVIEW

Answer the following questions with a partner or your classmates.

1. In what ways do you think the world of work is changing?

2. If you could choose to work either at an office or at home, which would you pick? Why? What are some of the advantages and disadvantages of working from home rather than at an office?

3. Look at the title of this chapter. What does *distributed* mean? What is a *workforce*? What do you think "the distributed workforce" is?

Two young men conduct business hanging from trees!

VOCABULARY PREVIEW

CD 2, TR 7

A **Read through the sentences below, which are missing vocabulary from the lecture. Listen to the sentences and write the missing words in the blanks.**

1. Employees may be based in a traditional office; or they might work from home— so-called _____; or they could be _____ employees, such as salespeople.

2. Employees working outside of the office need access from remote locations to company _____ and to stay connected with the use of _____ technology.

3. Full-time employees often expect _____ such as health insurance, and they might be difficult to _____.

4. It is not yet understood what impact a distributed workforce is having on the _____ yet vital development of a business culture.

5. How can group _____ be developed and maintained when face-to-face meetings are rare or _____?

6. How dependent are qualities such as loyalty and _____ behavior on personal relationships that are established through face-to-face contact?

7. Can personal relationships truly evolve across a distributed workforce, where much of the work is conducted in a _____ rather than physical environment?

8. When workers are available 24–7, it can lead to a _____ of the line between work and personal life.

9. In a _____ world, there is no _____.

10. Since the Industrial _____, the workplace has been where a large proportion of the adult population spends much of its time.

B **Check the spelling of the vocabulary words with your teacher. Discuss the meanings of these words and any other unfamiliar words in the sentences.**

PREDICTIONS

Think about the questions in the Topic Preview on page 46 and the sentences you heard in the Vocabulary Preview. Write three questions that you think will be answered in the lecture. Share your questions with your classmates.

NOTETAKING PREPARATION

Using Intonation to Identify New Main Points

A lecturer who has completed a main point and is ready to move on to a new point will often use very marked falling intonation, followed by a long pause.

The technology is here and it's here to **stay**. [long pause]

Signal words and phrases such as *next*, *another*, and *on the other hand* also indicate that the lecturer is moving from one main point to another. Often these signal words have strong rising intonation.

. . . and it's here to stay. [long pause] **On the oth**er hand . . .

The combination of marked falling intonation, a long pause, and a rising signal word should alert you to the fact that a new main point is about to be introduced.

CD 2, TR 8

A **Listen to the intonation in these sentences from the lecture. Has the lecturer finished talking about one main point and is now about to introduce a new one? Circle *a* or *b*.**

The lecturer will

1. a. introduce a new point   b. continue with same point

2. a. introduce a new point   b. continue with same point

3. a. introduce a new point   b. continue with same point

CD 2, TR 9

B **Listen to the sentences. This time you will hear how the lecturer continues and if a new main point is introduced. As you listen, check and see if you chose the correct answers in A above.**

FIRST LISTENING

CD 2, TR 10

Listen to the lecture and number the slides on this page and the next in the order they would be shown during the lecture. Write the number of the slide on the line provided and answer the question to the right of the slide.

The Distributed Workforce

Geography

Working arrangements

Technology

Slide #_____

What is a *distributed workforce*?

Advantages

Employers
- Local workforce
- Flexibility

Employees
- Location
- Schedule

Slide #_____

A distributed workforce has what obvious advantage to a global business?

Impact on Society

Humans as
social beings

Face-to-face
interaction

Work/Private life

Slide #_____

What do some distance
workers feel about
the loss of informal
social networks?

Disadvantages

Employers
- Impact on
  business culture

Employees
- 24–7 availability
- Lack of job
  security

Slide #_____

What problem can the
blurring of the line
between work and
personal life lead to?

Importance of Technology

Remote access

Communications
technology

Slide #_____

How important is
technology to a
business with a
distributed workforce?

SECOND LISTENING

Now that you've listened to the lecture once, listen to it again and take notes. Write on a separate piece of paper.

THIRD LISTENING

You will hear parts of the lecture again. Look through your notes as you listen. A notetaking mentor will discuss the notes. Circle the answer that is closest to the notes you took, and put a check (✓) next to the notes that the mentor wrote.

Part 1

1. a.

Wrkers ++
1. tech → wrk fr anywhere
2. indep contrct – + contrl wrk lives

b.

Benefits to wrkers
1. Tech make poss wrk to wrker, not wrker to job
2. stay close to fam & friends
3. indep contrac – + contrl wrk lives

Part 2

2. a.

Distance wrkrs

b.

Office wrkers

c.

Infrml support NWs

3. a.

Distance wrkrs
1. no offce → loss of soc NW
↓
isolation & ↓ support
2. + freedm BUT blur prvt/work

b.

Distance wrkrs
1. no offce → loss of soc NW
2. isolation & ↓ support
3. + freedm
4. xtra hrs eve & wkends

c.

Distance wrkrs
1. no offce → loss of soc NW
↓
isolation & ↓ support
2. blur bet. prvt/work
3. xtra hrs. eve & wkends

Part 3

4. a.

Flex Cost – Disadv
1. job sec (temp wrkrs/consul) – no ben (EX health ins)
2. Telecomm ↑ work, ↓ pay than offc wrkrs

b.

Disadv – Wrkrs
1. –job sec (temp wrkrs/consul)
2. no ben (EX health ins)
3. Telecomm ↑ work, ↓ pay than offc wrkrs

CD 2, TR 13

ACCURACY CHECK

You will hear questions about the lecture. Answer each question by referring to the notes that you took while listening to the lecture.

1. a. a business person
    b. a globally connected worker
    c. an office worker

2. a. a 24–7, globally connected world
    b. technological change and globalization
    c. a trend in the evolution of work

3. a. Most workers are telecommuters.
    b. Most employees don't have offices.
    c. Working arrangements vary.

4. a. workers' knowledge of local culture
    b. decreased cost of employing workers
    c. lower travel costs

5. a. flexibility
    b. better pay
    c. not having to relocate

6. a. less job security
    b. being able to terminate workers
    c. the impact on group cohesion

7. a. lack of flexibility
    b. fewer jobs being available
    c. work-related stress

8. a. better working conditions
    b. social isolation of workers
    c. decreased worker productivity

ORAL SUMMARY

Use your notes to create an oral summary of the lecture with your partner. As you work together, add details to your notes that your partner included but you had missed.

DISCUSSION

Discuss the following questions with a classmate or in a small group.

1. What are some potential advantages or disadvantages of a distributed workforce that were not mentioned in the lecture?

2. Do you think that the growth of a distributed workforce is likely to be better for employers or for employees? Why?

3. The lecturer raises a question about how group cohesion can be developed and maintained when many workers never meet face-to-face. What do you think? How can this be done?

4. Of the various employment arrangements discussed in the lecture—consulting, mobile work, telecommuting, temporary work, traditional office-based work—which do you prefer? Why?

PRE-READING

The following Reading is about the impact that virtual reality games are having on the business world. Before you read, answer the following questions. Share your answers with a classmate.

1. What are virtual reality games? Do you play any virtual reality games such as *Second Life*?

2. How do you think businesses can use virtual reality games to develop and promote real-world products and services?

READING

Now read the article.

"Second Life," Other Virtual Worlds Reshaping Human Interaction

Every day millions of personal computer (PC) gamers plug into online worlds. In the game *Second Life*, online entrepreneurs can buy and sell digital real estate, create their own lines of clothing and clothing accessories, and hold virtual concerts, lectures, and sporting events. Now, as the game has grown in popularity, many corporations are eager to follow the lead of independent retailers in becoming part of the phenomenon.

Observers say that someday virtual worlds such as *Second Life* could reshape global commerce and perhaps even the way people interact over the Internet. "Imagine a future where virtual reality and the real world blend together," said Edward Castronova, associate professor of telecommunications at Indiana University in Bloomington. "It is a real possibility, and it just takes an ordinary PC."

The popularity of MMORPGs (massively multiplayer online role-playing games), which mix real and unreal worlds, is one of the main factors shaping this digital revolution. One of the most popular games, *World of Warcraft*, "is played by about 7 million members worldwide, and on any given day there are at least a few million players online," Castronova said.

Second Life, created by San Francisco, California–based Linden Lab, uses the same concept as MMORPGs. It offers a virtual environment where people—as avatars—can interact in real time. But unlike *Warcraft*, which focuses mostly on fighting monsters and completing quests, *Second Life* is built and owned entirely by its nearly 900,000 residents.

According to Castronova, the real impact of virtual worlds is the daily creation and trade of electronic assets. For instance, a *Second Life* user can build a functional piano out of virtual building blocks with various physical and behavioral properties. Some members have created their own designer flying vehicles, while others have opened up skydiving operations or built entire airports.

A *Second Life* player points to her avatar.

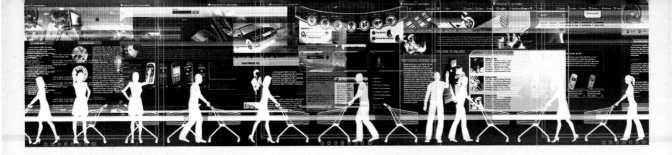

Second Life assigns intellectual property rights for all objects to their creators, meaning that the virtual objects can be sold or traded within the environment. Avatars earn an in-game currency called Linden Dollars—money that has an exchange rate and can be traded for hard cash in the real world. According to one estimate, players spend an average of $350,000 (U.S.) a day, or $130 million a year, according to Reuters.

Jerry Paffendorf is a futurist for the virtually based firm, Electric Sheep Company. Paffendorf and 25 others in the company all earn their living off virtual worlds, mostly *Second Life*. "It's a full-time job," he said. "We're the largest such team in *Second Life*."

The company also facilitates trade through a Web site called SLBoutique, an Amazon.com–like marketplace for user-created content in *Second Life*. A few products and services have already established brand recognition in the game, and it is entirely possible for such virtual brands to someday actually be sold in real-world operations, Paffendorf says. "Firms could prototype and test products inside a virtual environment," he explained.

It's an intriguing thought that virtual products that have been conceived, patented, tested, bought, and sold in an online game environment might one day become real products sold in the real world.

DISCUSSION

Discuss these questions with a classmate.

1. The article talks about how virtual worlds are "reshaping human interaction." What are some of the ways that human interaction is being reshaped in the workplace as discussed in the article and the lecture?

2. Given what you learned in the lecture, what are some potential advantages to employers of using virtual environments such as *Second Life* for business purposes? The disadvantages?

3. What are some of the potential advantages to employees of using a virtual environment for business purposes? The disadvantages?

RESEARCH PROJECT

Individually or in a group, research one of the following topics. Write a short paper on the topic or plan and present a group presentation to inform the class about the topic.

1. Workforce trends in your country or another country in which you are interested

2. Companies that are using *Second Life* for business purposes

3. Innovative workplace designs, for example, open-plan office space and the use of the "third space," such as coffee shops and airport terminals, as work spaces

4. The ways some workers are trying to reduce their environmental impact through their job choices

CHAPTER 6

Age and Work

The Graying of the Workforce

Answer the following questions with a partner or your classmates.

1. Look at the title of this chapter and the photograph. What trend do you think "the graying of the workforce" refers to?

2. At what age do people typically retire in your culture? Is it common for people who are older than 65 to continue working? Is there a mandatory retirement age?

3. Who is the oldest person you know who is still working?

Old man working in his paddy field located at Alor Setar, Kedah, Malaysia

VOCABULARY PREVIEW

CD 3, TR 1

A Read through the sentences below, which are missing vocabulary from the lecture. Listen to the sentences and write the missing words in the blanks.

1. The human _____ is also increasing: the National Institute on Aging reports that most countries show a steady increase in _____.

2. A falling _____ in countries with advanced economies has contributed to a rapid increase in the age of the world's population.

3. The reasons for the _____ birthrate require a bit of explanation.

4. The need for cheap labor to work the land, coupled with high infant _____, made large families advantageous.

5. During industrialization, there was a population _____ from rural to urban areas.

6. Advances in _____ technology allowed couples to take a more active role in planning their families.

7. In many developed nations, the birthrate has now fallen to below _____ levels.

8. The _____ rate in many European countries is now less than 1.5 children per woman.

9. The elderly support _____ is calculated by dividing the number of working-age people by the number of people 65 or older.

10. A second impact is caused by just the opposite _____, the large number of baby boomers who are and will be retiring at the same time, taking with them knowledge and _____ that will be difficult to replace over the short term.

11. _____ can occur when workers with such widely different life experiences and attitudes toward work interact.

12. Some companies have had to _____ back expansion due to a lack of workers.

B Check the spelling of the vocabulary words with your teacher. Discuss the meanings of these words and any other unfamiliar words in the sentences.

PREDICTIONS

Think about the questions in the Topic Preview on page 55 and the sentences you heard in the Vocabulary Preview. Write three questions that you think will be answered in the lecture. Share your questions with your classmates.

NOTETAKING PREPARATION

Showing Cause and Effect

Listen for cues that show a lecturer is expressing a cause/effect relationship between ideas. Make sure your notes reflect this relationship clearly by using the symbols below.

Cues to listen for ([C] = cause; [E] = effect)	Notes (∴ = therefore)
[C] *brings about / contributes to / results in / leads to* [E] [C] *affects / means (that) / makes / allows* [E] [C] *so* [E] *Due to* [C], [E] [C] *therefore* [E] *Because of* [C], [E] *As a result of* [C], [E]	[C] → [E] pop ↓ → oldr wrkrs ↑ [C] ∴ [E] pop ↓ ∴ oldr wrkrs ↑
[E] *because* [C] *The reason for* [E] *is* [C] [E] *is the result of* [C] [E] *is brought about by / is caused by* [C]	[E] b/c [C] oldr wrkrs ↑ b/c pop ↓ [E] ← [C] oldr wrkrs ↑ ← pop ↓

Ⓐ Look at the notes below. Match the note with the sentence. Circle *a* or *b*.

1. Wrk chngs b/c pop chngs of wf
   a. Today, we are going to talk about a change in the world of work that has been brought about by changes in the makeup of the population of the workforce.
   b. Today, we are going to talk about a change in the world of work that has contributed to changes in the makeup of the population of the workforce.

2. Hist fac → aging of pop
   a. I will explain historical factors that are the result of the aging of the population.
   b. I will explain historical factors that have contributed to the aging of the population.

3. ↓ b'rate adv econ & + med care → ↑ lifespan ∴ older wf
   a. Two basic trends—a falling birthrate in countries with advanced economies, and improvements in medical care—have contributed to an increased lifespan, leading to an older workforce.
   b. Two basic trends—a falling birthrate in countries with advanced economies, and improvements in medical care—are the result of an increased lifespan and an older workforce.

🔊
CD 3, TR 2
Ⓑ Listen to sentences from the lecture and take notes. Use the symbols in the box to express the relationship between cause and effect.

1. _____

2. _____

FIRST LISTENING
CD 3, TR 3

Listen to the lecture and number the slides on this page and the next in the order they would be shown during the lecture. Write the number of the slide on the line provided and answer the question to the right of the slide.

Elderly Support Ratio

I. Definition

II. Decline: Some statistics

III. Impact of decline

Slide #_____

What is the worldwide elderly support ratio predicted to be by 2050?

Population Changes → Graying of the Workforce

I. Population facts
   A. WHO
   B. National Institute on Aging

Slide #_____

By how much has the number of people aged 60 and over increased since 1980?

Reasons for Aging Population

I. Medical improvements

II. Changes in birthrate
    A. Industrial Revolution
    B. Start of WWII
    C. Post WWII baby boom
    D. Mid-1960s
    E. Today

Slide #_____

Did the birthrate increase or decrease during the Industrial Revolution?

Future?

I. Longer working life

II. Workplace changes

Slide #_____

What is likely to happen in the future if the population growth rate in advanced economies remains low?

Baby Boomers

I. Continued employment

II. Retirement

Slide #_____

What does the baby boomers staying in their jobs mean for young people entering the workforce?

SECOND LISTENING

Now that you've listened to the lecture once, listen to it again and take notes. Write on a separate piece of paper.

THIRD LISTENING

You will hear parts of the lecture again. Look through your notes as you listen. A notetaking mentor will discuss the notes. Circle the answer that is closest to the notes you took, and put a check (✓) next to the notes that the mentor wrote.

Part 1

1. a.

Bef IR – lg fam adv (+) b/c
1. need cheap labor (sm farm)
2. ↑ infant mort

b.

Lg fam adv (+) ← Bef IR
1. need for cheap labor (sm farm)
2. ↑ infant mort

c.

IR ∴ lg fam adv (+) b/c
1. need for cheap labor (sm farm)
2. ↑ infant mort

Part 2

2. a.

Indus → Pop shift → need lg fam ↓
Reprod tech adv ← ctrl fam size ∴ grad ↓ in b'rate

b.

Indus → Pop shift fr rur to urb → need lg fam ↓
&
Reprod tech adv → ctrl fam size
∴
grad ↓ in b'rate

Part 3

3. a.

Am wrkr med age ↑ fr 35 (1980) to 42 (2010) →
yng wrkrs diff finding jobs

b.

BB wrk past retire age* → yng wrkrs diff finding jobs

*Stat: Am wrkr med age ↑ fr 35 (1980) to 42 (2010)

CD 3, TR 6

ACCURACY CHECK

You will hear questions about the lecture. Answer each question by referring to the notes that you took while listening to the lecture.

1. a. by 2015
   b. by 2050
   c. in 20 to 50 years

2. a. Large families were common.
   b. Having children cost a lot.
   c. Most people lived in cities.

3. a. high infant mortality
   b. larger families
   c. medical advances

4. a. before World War II
   b. from 1946 to 1964
   c. in the mid 1960s

5. a. China
   b. Japan
   c. South Korea

6. a. Germany
   b. Italy
   c. Japan

7. a. 14 percent
   b. 22 percent
   c. 40 percent

8. a. a shortage of workers
   b. high youth unemployment
   c. retirement of baby boomers

ORAL SUMMARY

Use your notes to create an oral summary of the lecture with your partner. As you work together, add details to your notes that your partner included but you had missed.

DISCUSSION

Discuss the following questions with a classmate or in a small group.

1. The lecturer says that we live in a youth-oriented culture. Do you agree? Is it true of your culture? If so, how might this change in the future?

2. In what ways are workplaces not suited very well to aging workers? How could workplaces be designed to accommodate the aging workforce?

3. Which would you prefer: working with people of several different generations or working with people your own age? What are the advantages and disadvantages of each?

PRE-READING

The following Reading is about a workforce trend involving young Americans. Before you read, answer the following questions. Share your answers with a classmate.

1. Look at the title. What is the workforce trend that is discussed in the article?

2. Considering what you learned in the lecture about the employment situation facing young people today, why do you think some of them would be interested in farming as a career?

READING

Now read the article.

Why Are Young, Educated Americans Going Back to the Farm?

I am a 25-year-old college graduate with a degree from a respected university, and I spend my days on my knees, hands in the dirt, pulling weeds for a living. I am a farm intern, and I am not alone. Across the country, college students and graduates like myself, many with little or no farming background, are working for almost nothing in exchange for a little instruction in running a farm.

Young urban gardener with produce

John English, Web site manager for the National Agriculture Information Service farm internship bulletin board, said that postings there have jumped by around 500 per year for the last five years, as more small farms are established and need the cheap labor that interns provide.

Farming is difficult: There are endless chores and backbreaking physical labor. For much of the twentieth century, most Americans tried to escape such a life by moving to the city. Why would we want to go back to the farm?

The reasons are varied. Some see farming as a way to avoid participating in a capitalist economy. They share a concern for social justice and the environment, coupled with a lack of faith that existing political structures can or will deal with those issues. Other farm interns are drawn to farming by a much simpler need: paying the rent. Because of the sudden popularity of farmer's markets—that is, small markets that sell locally grown fruits, vegetables, meat, and cheese, rather than food grown thousands of miles away—a farm can look like a strong business opportunity to many young people. This is particularly true for the unemployed and those working at unfulfilling post-college jobs.

Interns interested in someday entering these growing markets must understand that when starting out they will probably earn very little. Kirk Wilson, 27, an intern at the Living Farm, earns $80 per week for his work, plus free housing and meals. Even this is more than many farms can offer. But he said he likes working outdoors and seeing things grow, and is learning the skills to run a small farm of his own someday. Having spent endless hours job hunting, Wilson also knows what he's not missing.

"I mean, am I gonna make $10 an hour for the rest of my life?" he asked. "If that's the case, then coming here and having no rent, room and board, and making $16 a day . . . I'm completely fine with that."

Increased competition for such low pay raises a potential problem, one that other attractive but low-paying fields, like journalism, are facing: Those with bills to pay or families to support, who cannot afford to accept farm wages, may be squeezed out, leaving the best farm jobs to those whose financial safety net (parents, trust fund, etc.) allows them to work for nothing.

In fact, it's likely that many of today's interns will decide to leave farming, going back to school or taking city jobs. After all, there are many obstacles to becoming a successful farmer; making a living on a small farm is as hard today as it has ever been. Government data suggests that the number of hobby farms—those earning less than $10,000 per year—increased slightly in 2010. At the same time, the number of midsized farms—those that earn between $10,000 and $100,000—decreased. And yet, the formation of groups like the National Young Farmers Coalition suggests that many small farms plan to keep going. Their goal seems less about getting rich than simply surviving, and perhaps changing a small part of the world in the process.

DISCUSSION

Discuss these questions with a classmate.

1. What surprised or interested you most about the trend described in the article? Why?

2. What information from the lecture was exemplified in the article?

3. Thinking back to what you learned from the lecture, do you agree with the author that young Americans will continue to turn to farming in the future, or is this just a temporary trend?

RESEARCH PROJECT

Individually or in a group, research one of the following topics. Write a short paper on the topic or plan and present a group presentation to inform the class about the topic.

1. A comparison of salaries by age in your country or another country in which you are interested

2. Professions that are currently facing worker shortages

3. Age discrimination

4. The growth of hobby farms in the United States

An Actor and a Travel Writer

TOPIC PREVIEW

Andrew McCarthy is both an actor and a travel writer. What are some ways that people sometimes get started in each of these careers? Compare your answers with a partner.

Started in acting	Started in travel writing

VOCABULARY PREVIEW

A Read the definitions of these key words and phrases that you will hear during the video.

cut from the team removed as a player from a sports team because of less skill

reticent not willing to talk very much

kicked out of college forced to leave school, usually because of bad grades or bad behavior

role a character an actor plays in a play or a movie

supported me provided me with enough money to live on

genre a particular type of writing, music, movie, etc.

encounters meetings with people that you didn't plan

scene a short event in a play or movie

my life is transitioning what I do in life is changing to something new

B Work with a partner and discuss answers to the following questions.

1. Have you ever been on a sports team? Have ever been **cut from the team**?

2. How would you or your family feel if you **were kicked out of college**?

3. Are you a **reticent** person? What is a topic that you are **reticent** to talk about?

4. If you had a **role** in a movie, what **genre** would you like the movie to be? What type of **scenes** would you like to be in?

5. Have you ever had an **encounter** with someone that has helped you to **transition** to a new phase of your life?

6. Who **supports** you at the moment?

🖵 FIRST VIEWING

Watch the video, and then compare your first impressions with a partner. Talk about what you remember, what surprised you, and what interested you.

🖵 SECOND VIEWING

Watch the video again. Listen for the missing words and write them in the blanks.

1. And so I did, and that experience, I have to say, changed my _____.

2. And then suddenly, I got jobs very quickly, and I was suddenly a 22-year-old _____.

3. So I started reading a lot of travel _____, and I thought it was a very interesting genre, you know.

4. I wasn't keeping a _____ in any way, but I would write little scenes of encounters I had with people.

5. I'll always be the _____ who was in *Pretty in Pink*, you know?

6. So it's given me _____ and opened _____ for me and, you know, so it's just part of my story.

Andrew McCarthy

📺 THIRD VIEWING

**Take notes below to answer the interview questions as you watch the video.
Listen for cause-and-effect cues and use indentation.**

How did acting enter your life? How did you become an actor? How did you get started?

So how did travel writing enter this equation?

When you look at your life do you feel like you're more an actor or a travel writer?

ORAL SUMMARY

**Use your notes to create an oral summary of the video with your partner. As
you work together, add details to your notes that your partner included but you
had missed.**

DISCUSSION

Discuss the following questions with a classmate or in a small group.

1. In what ways do you think Andrew McCarthy's career as a movie star is not typical?

2. Andrew says, "At a certain point in my life, when I was about 30, I looked up and
   said, 'Huh?'" What do you think he means?

3. In what ways do you think your working life is or will be different from Andrew
   McCarthy's? In what ways do you think it might be similar?

Communication

The Influence of Language, Culture, and Gender

Sticky notes with messages in the Times Square Information Center

Classroom Communication

Language and Culture in the Classroom

TOPIC PREVIEW

Answer the following questions with a partner or your classmates.

1. What kind of communication takes place in classrooms in your culture? For example, do students talk much with each other during class time? How and when do they communicate with their teacher?

2. How do students in your culture show respect for their teachers?

3. Do you think classroom communication is the same everywhere, or is it specific to a culture? Give examples to support your answer.

Sudanese school teacher in a classroom in Nyala, Darfur

VOCABULARY PREVIEW

CD 3, TR 7

A **Read through the sentences below, which are missing vocabulary from the lecture. Listen to the sentences and write the missing words in the blanks.**

1. Communication can take the form of talk, or it can take the form of _____, or nonverbal signals of one kind or another.

2. Many _____ study the topic of communication in general, and speech communication specifically, in order to learn how individuals send and _____ messages.

3. One area of research in _____ communication is the study of the influence of the _____, or environment, on the success or failure of communication.

4. When you are asked to picture a classroom in your _____ eye, what do you see?

5. The "classroom" as we know it, by the way, is a relatively recent _____.

6. In particular, culture influences the _____ that take place in the classroom setting, and the ways that students participate in the classroom _____.

7. Rituals are _____ procedures used to perform a certain act or to communicate a certain message.

8. In some graduate-level seminars in American universities, students do not make any physical signs when they want to speak; they state their ideas whenever they feel the _____.

9. North American students from families of European _____ are usually more talkative in class and more willing to state their opinions than are students of American Indian _____ or from Asian backgrounds.

10. The _____ in which teachers are held also varies from culture to culture.

B **Check the spelling of the vocabulary words with your teacher. Discuss the meanings of these words and any other unfamiliar words in the sentences.**

PREDICTIONS

Think about the questions in the Topic Preview on page 68 and the sentences you heard in the Vocabulary Preview. Write three questions that you think will be answered in the lecture. Share your questions with your classmates.

NOTETAKING PREPARATION

Recording Rhetorical Questions

In a lecture, the main points are often introduced as *rhetorical questions*. A rhetorical question is a question that the speaker does not expect the listener to answer. The question is a way to call attention to a main point that the lecturer will go on to develop.

Here are some examples of cues frequently used for rhetorical questions and their answers.

When . . . what do you . . . ?	Just what (exactly) is/are . . . ?
You probably . . .	The definition of . . .
But what do we mean by . . . ?	And what about . . . ?
Basically, . . .	Well, . . .

When you hear a rhetorical question in a lecture, be sure to record it. Use a simple abbreviation to label the question and answer.

Q = rhetorical question   A = answer

Put the question above the answer and use indentation to show the details, support, or explanation—in other words, the answer to the question. For example:

Lecture	**Notes**
But what do we mean by culture? Basically, culture provides us with a system of knowledge that allows us to communicate with others and teaches us how to interpret their verbal and nonverbal behavior.	Q: Wht is cult A: syst knowl for • comm ↔ others • interp vb & nonvb behv

A Rewrite the notes using the abbreviations *Q* and *A* and indentation.

> But wh ex is a clssrm? Ans influ by cult & incl teach/stud rel, how info tght and lrnd, how teach/stud comm

B Listen to a part of the lecture and complete the notes. A heading has been provided. Remember to use *Q* and *A* and indentation.

CD 3, TR 8

> Lang, cult, and comm in clssrms

FIRST LISTENING

CD 3, TR 9

Listen to the lecture and number the slides on this page and the next in the order they would be shown during the lecture. Write the number of the slide on the line provided and answer the question to the right of the slide.

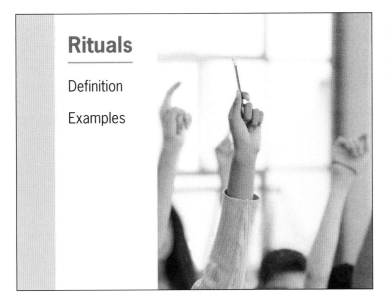

Rituals

Definition

Examples

Slide #_____

How do Jamaican students signal that they want to answer a question?

What Is a Classroom?

How information is taught and learned

Teacher/student communication

Teacher/student relationship

Slide #_____

What influences the image that people have of a classroom?

Language, Culture, and Communication

Definition of communication

Verbal and nonverbal

Intercultural communication
  • Setting

Slide #_____

How do people communicate their thoughts, feelings, and intentions to others?

Treatment of Teachers

Asia

Germany

Israel

Slide #_____

In which country or region do students sometimes criticize their teachers in class?

Classroom Participation

European American

American Indian

Asian

Slide #_____

Which North American students are the more talkative in class?

◀» SECOND LISTENING

CD 3, TR 10

Now that you have listened to the lecture once, listen to it again and take notes. Write on a separate piece of paper.

◀» THIRD LISTENING

CD 3, TR 11

You will hear parts of the lecture again. Look through your notes as you listen. A notetaking mentor will discuss the notes. Circle the answer that is closest to the notes you took, and put a check (✓) next to the notes that the mentor wrote.

Part 1

1. a.

> Q: Wht is cult?
> A: Sys of know that...
> • allows comm w/ others
> • teaches how to intrprt ppl's v and nv beh
> • influ how ppl interact

b.

> Q: Wht is cult?
> A: Term usd in diff ways
> • sys of know that allows comm w/ others
> • teaches how to intrprt ppl's v and nv beh
> • influ how ppl interact

c.

> Q: What do we mean by culture?
> A: Basic – cult provide syst of know that allows us to comm w/ others and teaches us how to interpret their verb and nonverb behav – influences how ppl interact

Part 2

2. a.

> Q: Wht r rituals?
> A: Sys proc
> ↙ ↘
> prfrm act   comm msg

b.

> Dictionary def of rituals = syst proc to prfrm act or comm msg. Many rits in ed. T enters clssrm, st stand up

c.

> Q: Wht r rituals?
> A: Syst proced to prfrm act or comm msg many in educ
> ex: T enters clssrm, st stand up

Part 3

3. a.

> Q: How much r Ts respctd?
> A: Varies fr cult to cult
> • Asns – Ts sym of learn & cult
> • Ger – value T's opin so don't disagr w/ T in clss
> • Israel – can critic T

b.

> Q: How r Ts treated? How much r they respctd?
> A: Varies – Asns – Ts respctd – symbol of learn & cult Ger – don't disagr in clss Israel – can critic T

CD 3, TR 12

ACCURACY CHECK

You will hear questions about the lecture. Answer each question by referring to the notes that you took while listening to the lecture.

1. a. system of knowledge
   b. expected communication procedures
   c. a form of human behavior

2. a. a classroom ritual
   b. cross-cultural communication
   c. speech communication

3. a. being talkative in class
   b. correcting a teacher
   c. finger snapping

4. a. exchange ideas with classmates
   b. explore issues for themselves
   c. speak only if the teacher speaks to them

5. a. The teacher is a symbol of learning.
   b. Teachers give their opinions.
   c. Teachers are criticized.

6. a. Criticizing a teacher is acceptable.
   b. Contradicting a teacher is considered rude.
   c. It is acceptable to correct a teacher.

7. a. Asians and American Indians
   b. European Americans and Germans
   c. Americans and Israelis

8. a. student-teacher classroom interaction
   b. relationships outside of class
   c. nonverbal communication

ORAL SUMMARY

Use your notes to create an oral summary of the lecture with your partner. As you work together, add details to your notes that your partner included but you had missed.

DISCUSSION

Discuss the following questions with a classmate or in a small group.

1. The lecturer says that teachers in some cultures are honored members of society. Is this true in your culture? If so, how is this esteem demonstrated? If not, how are teachers seen in your culture?

2. What are some classroom rituals in your culture that were not mentioned in the lecture? Are they similar to those in other cultures with which you are familiar?

3. The classroom rituals discussed in the lecture were mostly nonverbal. Can you think of any verbal classroom rituals?

PRE-READING

The following Reading is about communicating in a third language. Before you read, answer the following questions. Share your answers with a classmate.

1. Look at the title of the article. What is a *lingua franca*? Based on the title and the photograph, what do you think the article will be about?

2. Do you think that your personality changes when you speak English? Discuss any changes you have noticed and talk about what the reasons might be.

READING

Now read the article.

Love that Lingua Franca

Michiko, the young Japanese woman I'm sharing a seat with on a bus near Tokyo, speaks a shy, hesitant English. I resign myself to a couple of hours filled with awkward, polite English. But then something unexpected happens. Grasping for a subject to talk about with her, I spot the headline on the cover of a local tourism brochure, written in Japanese and English. Japanese has Chinese characters in its writing system and I can read Chinese, so I immediately notice that the characters for the Japanese word "*Chiba*" mean "One Thousand Leaves."

Pointing to the brochure, I turn to Michiko and say: "*Chiba* means one thousand leaves."

"Yes!" she responds, then adds in a French accent that is much better than mine, "*Milles feuilles*—A thousand leaves." "*Mais alors*—So," I say, "*vous parlez français*—you speak French." "No," she answers, and, once again in a perfect accent, says "*Hablo español*—I speak Spanish." Fantastic! "*Yo también*—me, too," I tell her. We've found common ground, and race into an extended conversation.

As shy as Michiko is in English, she's confident and funny when she speaks in Spanish. It has been observed that we often change personalities when we switch languages. I don't speak any Japanese, so I don't know what Michiko is like in her mother tongue. In the third tongue of Spanish, however, we blast past not just linguistic but cultural differences to have a real conversation.

This isn't the first time I've experienced the thrill of connecting with someone in a third-party tongue, which is what I call a common language that's nonnative to both speakers. Since I believe every traveler should speak other languages, I have spent years learning two myself, Spanish and Cantonese. When I'm in Madrid or Guangzhou, I do my best to keep up with the rapid, slangy conversation of native speakers. I lean forward into the conversations and listen with all my concentration and heart, but after a while of struggling I become exhausted and frustrated, and soon give up.

The not-native-to-either-party language is like a neutral territory, a halfway point where the joys and difficulties of communication are shared equally. I speak more slowly, knowing that my listeners may not "hear" me like a native; they do the same. As a traveler, I want my words to bring me closer to people, so I grab every chance I get to use that most democratic and liberating language of all, the third tongue. Sometimes just finding a third tongue can be an adventure. One day in India's northern state of Rajasthan, I suddenly heard a very familiar rhythm of sounds. I turned and found four European women discussing the architectural details of a temple in Spanish. I greeted them with an "¡Hola!" and we ended up having lunch together.

Cenotaph tombs in India

Back in the bus with Michiko, we finally arrive at our destination. We fall out of Spanish and back into our mother languages and our roles: the local person and the foreign tourist. Now, though, we know the third tongue will be there when we need it.

DISCUSSION

Discuss the following questions with a classmate or in a small group.

1. In what ways does the information in the article provide support for the ideas introduced in the lecture regarding cross-cultural communication?

2. Does anything in the article refute the ideas introduced in the lecture? If so, what? Be specific.

3. The article addresses the advantages of communicating in a third tongue. Using what you have learned from the lecture, discuss the possible disadvantages.

RESEARCH PROJECT

Individually or in a group, research one of the following topics. Write a short paper on the topic, or plan and present a presentation to inform the class about the topic.

1. Classroom communication patterns in your culture or in another culture in which you have an interest

2. Nonverbal communication in your culture as compared to another culture in which you have an interest

3. A comparison of business communication patterns in two cultures

4. Another related topic that interests you or your group

Gender and Communication

Male–Female Conversation as Cross-cultural Communication

TOPIC PREVIEW

Answer the following questions with a partner or your classmates.

1. In your culture, what kinds of games do little girls play? Do little boys play the same kinds of games? If not, how are the games of boys and girls different?

2. Look at the title of the chapter. Is male–female communication a type of cross-cultural communication? Explain.

3. In your culture, is there a difference in the way that men and women communicate in different situations, for example, in a business meeting, at a party, in a class seminar or small class, at a family dinner? Explain your answers.

VOCABULARY PREVIEW

CD 3, TR 13

A **Read through the sentences below, which are missing vocabulary from the lecture. Listen to the sentences and write the missing words in the blanks.**

1. Boys learn to be _____ and girls learn to be _____ as they grow to be men and women.

2. Children learn how to talk to other children or adults, and how to have conversations, not only from their parents, but also from their _____.

3. Deborah Tannen and other researchers on this topic have found that young boys tend to play outside the home rather than in, and they play in large groups that are _____ structured.

4. It is by giving orders and making the other boys play by the rules that boys achieve higher and more _____ status in the play group.

5. Boys also achieve _____ by taking center _____.

6. The boys were making slingshots; the girls were making _____.

7. The girls making the rings were more _____.

8. As a result of our cultural _____, we learn norms of behavior and patterns of communication that are often gender based, and sometimes gender _____.

9. Well, perhaps it is our social concept of what is feminine and what is masculine that reinforces the _____ that women talk more than men, and even causes these different patterns of communication.

10. This means that a Zulu wife must _____ and find other ways to say these things.

B **Check the spelling of the vocabulary words with your teacher. Discuss the meanings of these words and any other unfamiliar words in the sentences.**

PREDICTIONS

Think about the questions in the Topic Preview on page 77 and the sentences you heard in the Vocabulary Preview. Write three questions that you think will be answered in the lecture. Share your questions with your classmates.

NOTETAKING PREPARATION

Contrast Cues and Charts

Listen for cues that show a lecturer is expressing a contrast, or difference, between two things. Make sure your notes reflect this relationship clearly by using the symbols below.

Cues to listen for	Notes		
different / differently / difference	$\neq$	DIFF	
less / fewer (than) / not as . . . as	$<$	$-$	$\downarrow$
-er / more (than)	$>$	$+$	$\uparrow$
on the other hand / however	$\downarrow$	BUT	
the (exact) opposite	$\neq$		

A chart with side-by-side lists helps make contrasts clear. You can organize your notes in a chart after the lecture. Use symbols for contrasts and indents for main ideas and supporting details.

Boys: lrg grps outside, ↑ hierarch-leader-ordrs ≠ Girls: sm grps or 2s,
↓ hierarch. Ex: hopsc, jump rp, take turn–suggs not ordr

    <u>Girls</u>   <u>Boys</u>
    • sm grps or 2s   • lrg grps
    • ↓ hierarch = take turn, suggs   • ↑ hierarch = leader, ordrs
         Ex: hopsc, jump rp

                                        • + outside

Use the same order in each column. If something is mentioned for only one of the things being compared, put that point at the end.

A On a separate piece of paper, reorganize the notes in the chart below to show comparisons in the same order, side-by-side.

<u>Boys</u>   <u>Girls</u>
    • + talk –joke, story   Games – no win/losers
    • + ordrs
    • dom conv—interr   Comm Styls
Games   • ↓ dir ordrs
    • win/losers   • ↑ suggs
    • + rules

B Listen to a part of the lecture for the notes below. Rewrite the notes as a chart.

CD 3, TR 14

Rsrch: MH Goodwin—comp boys/girls task. Boys=make slshot/Girls=jewlry/
Boys–hierarchy/lder tld what & how ≠ Girls–egal–ev suggs; list & accpt sugg

CD 3, TR 15

🔊 FIRST LISTENING

Listen to the lecture and number the slides on this page and the next in the order they would be shown during the lecture. Write the number of the slide on the line provided and answer the question to the right of the slide.

Social Concepts Reinforce Stereotyping

Feminine/Masculine behavior

Example from Zulu culture

Slide #_____

What are women taught about how to be feminine?

Learning to Communicate Through Play

Boys' play
- large groups
- hierarchy

Girls' play
- small groups
- take turns

Slide #_____

How do boys achieve status when playing?

Stereotypes

Talk time

Interruption

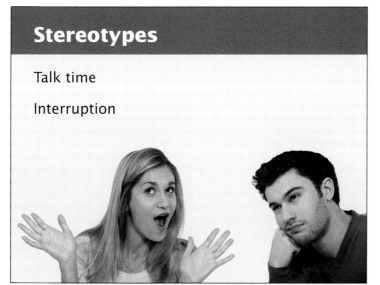

Slide #_____

Are the stereotypes about how much women talk accurate?

Gender: Definition

Differences in male–female communication

How communication patterns are learned

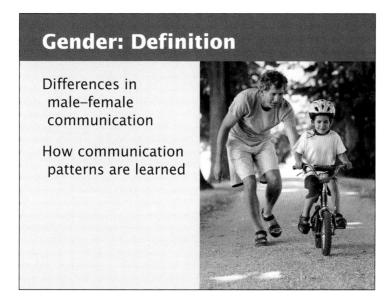

Slide #_____

How are communication patterns learned?

Research Findings— Communication in Professional Settings

Eakins' study

Simeone study

Slide #_____

What was the main finding of the Eakins' study?

SECOND LISTENING

Now that you've listened to the lecture once, listen to it again and take notes.
Write on a separate piece of paper.

THIRD LISTENING

You will hear parts of the lecture again. Look through your notes as you listen. A
notetaking mentor will discuss the notes. Circle the answer that is closest to the
notes you took, and put a check (✓) next to the notes that the mentor wrote.

Part 1

1. a.

who tlks & intrpt more?
stereotype = women > men
BUT
reality = men > women

b.

The stereotype is woman
take center stage by
talking & interrupt but
research show opposite
is true

c.

Men	Women
talk & intrpt	talk & intrpt
<women	<men
(stereo)	(true)

Part 2

2. a.

Male profs	F'male profs
Res #1 (Eakins) 7 univ fac mtgs	Res #1
• talkd 10.66–17.07 sec	• talkd 3–10 sec
Res #2 (Simeone) univ dept mtgs	Res #2
• 46% said they talkd	• 15% said they talked

b.

Res #1	Res #2
Eakins	Simeone
7 univ fac mtgs; timed who talked	univ dept mtgs – who said they talkd?
male prof: 10.66–17.07 sec	male prof: 46%
f'male " : 3–10 sec	f'male " : 15%

Part 3

3. a.

Men	Women
cult says tlking/intrpt ok	cult says tlking/intrpt NOT ok
not critic for tlking/intrpt	critic for tlking/intrpt, even if just a little

b.

Cult Expec	
Masculine role	Feminine role
expected = ↑ talk & intrpt	expected = ↓ talk & intrpt
SO	SO
↓ critic, even if they do it ↑	↑ critic, even if they do it ↓

ACCURACY CHECK

CD 3, TR 18

You will hear questions about the lecture. Answer each question by referring to the notes that you took while listening to the lecture.

1. a. from conversations
   b. from brothers and sisters
   c. from parents and other children

2. a. They play together a lot.
   b. They prefer same-sex groups.
   c. They rarely play together.

3. a. Girls are less hierarchical.
   b. Girls don't care who wins.
   c. Girls enjoy team sports more.

4. a. Girls suggest, but boys order.
   b. Girls talk more.
   c. Boys argue more.

5. a. to make others laugh
   b. to make friends
   c. to achieve status

6. a. a little girl playing hopscotch
   b. a little boy making a slingshot
   c. a little boy or girl playing house

7. a. Women are encouraged to talk.
   b. Men talk and interrupt more.
   c. Women talk and interrupt more.

8. a. family relationships
   b. gender in communication
   c. an unequal society

ORAL SUMMARY

Use your notes to create an oral summary of the lecture with your partner. As you work together, add details to your notes that your partner included but you had missed.

DISCUSSION

Discuss the following questions with a classmate or in a small group.

1. What stereotypes do you have in your culture about how women communicate? About men? Do you think these stereotypes are an accurate description of male and female communication patterns? Why or why not?

2. What are some of the differences in the ways that women and men communicate in your culture?

3. Based on what was said in the lecture, do you think that Deborah Tannen would support single-sex education—that is, having all-boy and all-girl schools? Why or why not?

4. In your culture, are single-sex schools common? Would you prefer your children to be educated in a single-sex school, or a mixed-sex one? Why?

PRE-READING

The following Reading is about a study on group intelligence. Before you read, answer the following questions. Share your answers with a classmate.

1. Look at the title of the article. Write two things that you expect to learn from the article.

2. Based on what you learned in the lecture, do you think groups with more female than male members would be better at thought-based tasks such as visual puzzles?

READING

Now read the article.

Smarter Teams Are More Sensitive, Have More Women?

Being smart doesn't matter much if you're working in a group, according to the first study to calculate collective intelligence—a group's ability to succeed at a variety of tasks.

Surprisingly, in a team an individual's intelligence has little to do with success in thought-based tasks such as visual puzzles and negotiating over limited resources, a set of recent experiments found. Instead, a group is more successful if it contains people who are more "socially sensitive"—in this case meaning they're better able to read emotions from people's faces.

That also explains why groups with more women—who score higher on tests of social sensitivity—were more likely to excel, said study leader Anita Williams Woolley, an expert in collective intelligence at Carnegie Mellon University in Pittsburgh. Particularly intelligent groups also had more people who took turns speaking, according to the study, published in the journal *Science*. "There's such a focus on individual intelligence and individual accomplishment, especially in western culture," she said. "As our world becomes flatter and more interconnected, it's not as important to consider what an individual can do by themselves but what they can do collectively."

Calculating Collective Intelligence

Individual intelligence is measured by the ability of a person to do multiple tasks well, Woolley said. To see if the same would be true of groups, Woolley and

colleagues recruited 699 volunteers and first measured each person's intelligence and social sensitivity using standard psychological tests.

The volunteers were then split into groups of two to five and asked to do some simple tasks, such as solving a visual puzzle. The results revealed that certain groups were better at all types of tasks, which is the "primary evidence for the notion of collective intelligence," Woolley said. Next, the groups were each asked to perform more complex tasks, which included playing a video game against an imaginary opponent and solving a research-and-development problem. As suspected, the groups' collective intelligence scores from the first round of tests predicted how they'd do on the complex experiments, Woolley said.

Findings May Benefit Real-World Groups

This ability to predict group success may offer guidance in real-life situations—especially as more decisions in fields such as business and the military are made in consensus-based settings, she said. For instance, knowing a group's collective intelligence could be vital in a high-risk situation where poor performance could mean failure, such as starting a new business.

Group Smarts Rooted in Animal Kingdom

Group intelligence may also be rooted in the past. For instance, "You can't be really good at hunting but not good at gathering," Woolley said. "Figuring out how to more flexibly deploy the skills available through members of groups would be associated with survival."

Likewise, Woolley said, the study is evidence that human societies may function better in groups. "It's no mistake that some of the earlier work on collective intelligence does borrow from the animal kingdom." For instance, "ants are simple creatures but collectively can accomplish things that are amazing."

DISCUSSION

Discuss these questions with a classmate.

1. How does the information in the article provide support for the ideas introduced in the lecture regarding male–female patterns of communication?

2. Did anything in the article surprise you because it seemed different from what you heard in the lecture? If so, what? Be specific.

3. The study's findings seem to suggest that strong communication skills, both verbal and nonverbal, are related to intelligence. Based on what you have learned from the lecture, why do you think that might be true?

RESEARCH PROJECT

Individually or in a group, research one of the following topics. Write a short paper on the topic, or plan and present a group presentation to inform the class about the topic.

1. The role of communication in collective intelligence (also known as *swarm intelligence*)

2. Male and female communication patterns in Zulu culture

3. Classroom communication in your culture or in another culture in which you have an interest

4. Another related topic that interests you or your group

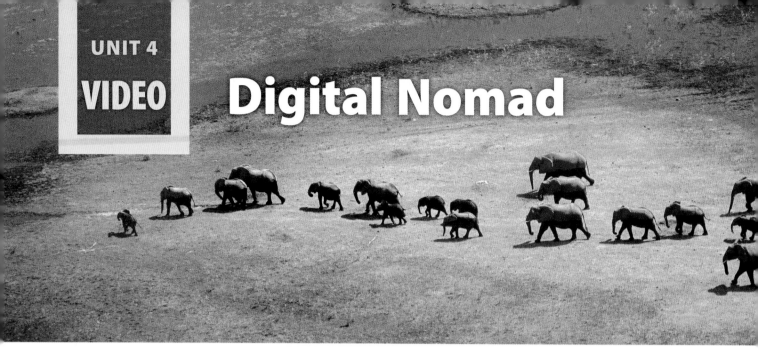

UNIT 4

VIDEO **Digital Nomad**

TOPIC PREVIEW

Twitter is a form of communication in which people write short messages, called *Tweets.* **Answer these questions about Tweets with a partner.**

1. What do you know about Tweets, and how to write them?

2. Do you have a Twitter account? If so, what do you Tweet about?

3. Can you name any famous people who Tweet? What sorts of things do they Tweet about?

4. Do you think Tweeting is easy, fun, or silly? Why or why not?

VOCABULARY PREVIEW

Ⓐ Read the definitions of these vocabulary words and phrases that you will hear during the video.

a real-time narrative a story told at the same time that an event is happening

memoir a written story of the events in someone's life

a pro a person with professional skill at doing something

tips pieces of useful advice

eclipse cover or block something that is more important

a wildebeest carcass the dead body of a large African animal with curving horns, also called a *gnu*

there was no reception cell phones couldn't operate because there was no signal

obsessed thinking about only one particular thing and not anything else

unplug periodically to take a break from using electronic devices sometimes

B Work with a partner and write in the blank the word from the box that best completes the sentence.

event	record	river	Tweets
explorers	remember	technology	video

1. The early _____ wrote **memoirs**, but modern writers like to write **real-time narratives**.

2. It is difficult to be **a pro** at writing _____.

3. There was **no reception** anywhere, except for one place, which was down by the _____, next to a **wildebeest carcass**.

4. It's possible to use modern _____ too much. Let me give you an important **tip**: _____ to **unplug periodically**.

5. Don't become so **obsessed** with trying to _____ an experience by writing or shooting _____ that you allow your obsession to **eclipse** your ability to experience the _____.

VIEWING

🖥 FIRST VIEWING

Watch the video, and then compare your first impressions with a partner. Talk about what you remember, what surprised you, and what interested you.

🖥 SECOND VIEWING

Watch the video again. Listen for the missing words and write them in the blanks.

1. Now this follows an ancient _____ form of poetry. But it's very short and it has all the great ingredients of a Tweet, of _____.

2. And I've Tweeted—not underwater, that doesn't work yet, but almost. I Tweeted in _____ time while flying a plane, in French.

3. And they always wanted to drive by the carcass, because the carcass for whatever _____ had coverage. So they could always _____ their e-mail and their Tweets whenever we got by the carcass.

A wildebeest

4. We take much better pictures than _____ do. We feel a place. We have these _____.

Complete these notes as you watch the video. Use abbreviations and symbols as necessary.

Use Twitter
- orig NG explorers – keep jurnl, wrt bk later = _____ mem
- A.E. – real time mem, _____

Lrning to Tweet (sent 5000 fr DC to Antarctica)
- Twitter = short _____ = 140 _____
- lrnd fr _____, eg Haiku (Jap) is _____
- set stage
- _____
- place
- _____
- character
- _____

Tips
1. be there
2. shar'g must not _____
   - EX journalists w
     - miss beauty & _____
     - no phone recp – 1 spot; obsessed & _____
3. if obsessed w _____ you _____
4. unplug, because _____

AFTER VIEWING

ORAL SUMMARY

Use your notes to create an oral summary of the video with your partner. As you work together, add details to your notes that your partner included but you had missed.

DISCUSSION

Discuss the following questions with a classmate or in a small group.

1. How is Andrew Evans similar to the first National Geographic explorers? How is he different?

2. Write a Tweet. Use Andrew's tips for writing a good Tweet. Remember, you can only use 140 characters or less.

3. What are Andrew Evans' tips for being a good digital nomad? Do you agree that people need to "unplug"? Why or why not?

4. Andrew says, "Never let sharing the experience eclipse having the experience." What does he mean? Do you think this is a problem? Give examples.

Biology

From Genetics to Genetic Engineering

Illustration showing the double helix of human DNA

The Origins of Genetics

Mendel and the Garden Pea Experiment

TOPIC PREVIEW

Answer the following questions with a partner or your classmates.

1. Why do people look the way they do? Why do you look similar to, but different from, your parents, brothers, and sisters?

2. Look at the title of this chapter. Can you guess who Mendel was and how his study of pea plants furthered our understanding of heredity and genetics?

3. How can an understanding of genetics help agriculture?

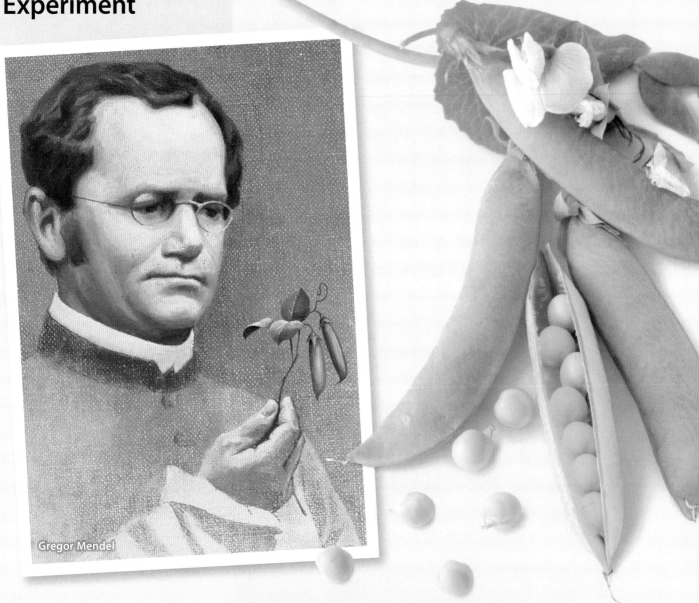

Gregor Mendel

VOCABULARY PREVIEW

CD 4, TR 1

A **Read through the sentences below, which are missing vocabulary from the lecture. Listen to the sentences and write the missing words in the blanks.**

1. _____ determine how every living creature on earth appears, how it functions, how it _____, and generally, how it behaves.

2. Inherited _____, or characteristics, are determined by _____ of genes that are different for every human being.

3. The scientists who study how genes are _____ and passed from one generation to the next are called _____.

4. I want to _____ and briefly examine the work of a _____ in biology, Gregor Mendel.

5. Mendel studied science at the University of Vienna, and there he learned how to use mathematics to try to explain natural _____.

6. When a variety of garden pea that had violet flowers was _____ with a variety that had white flowers, all the _____ surprisingly had only violet flowers.

7. Mendel applied his knowledge of mathematics and statistics to help him _____ the results of the _____ of the white-flowering and violet-flowering plants.

8. The pea plants could be _____ quickly, and with little effort.

9. We now know that genes are tiny _____ structures inside each cell that determine eye color, blood type, height, and so on.

10. A person may have a genetic _____ toward being overweight, but the person's actual weight will depend on a number of environmental _____.

B **Check the spelling of the vocabulary words with your teacher. Discuss the meanings of these words and any other unfamiliar words in the sentences.**

PREDICTIONS

Think about the questions in the Topic Preview on page 90 and the sentences you heard in the Vocabulary Preview. Write three questions that you think will be answered in the lecture. Share your questions with your classmates.

NOTETAKING PREPARATION

Anticipating and Recording Examples

In the course of a lecture, you will almost always hear examples that explain or reinforce an important point. Here is some language a lecturer might use to introduce an example:

For example, . . .   *. . . like . . .*   *Let me give you an example. . . .*
. . . including . . .   *. . . such as . . .*

When you hear a lecturer use any of these phrases, use one of the following abbreviations in your notes to show you are recording an example:

EX –   For ex –   e.g. –

Remember that examples support a main point.

- List them under the related main point in your notes.
- Indent them to show that they are less important than the main point.
- Leave extra room so that you can later add examples or details you may have missed.

A Look at the lecture notes below. With a partner, read the notes out loud as sentences. Think of some possible examples the lecturer might give. Write them on a separate paper.

1. Genes—passed dn – gener → gener – e.g. . . .

2. Many traits ≈ prnts' trts, e.g. . . .

3. We breed anmls to be better—For ex racehorse: > . . .

4. Garden pea: many traits w/ 2 diff forms – e.g. . . .

5. Pers cn hv genet tend to ovrwt, BUT also dep on environ: EX . . .

CD 4, TR 2
B Listen to the sentences from the lecture for the notes in **A** above. Write the examples that you hear in the space under the notes. Remember to indent. Compare the examples you heard with those you wrote on a separate paper. Were some of your predictions in **A** correct?

FIRST LISTENING

CD 4, TR 3

Listen to the lecture and number the slides on this page and the next in the order they would be shown during the lecture. Write the number of the slide on the line provided and answer the question to the right of the slide.

The Garden Pea Experiments

Thomas Knight
- Unexplained results

Gregor Mendel
- Repeated Knight
- Applied statistical analysis

Advantages of pea plant

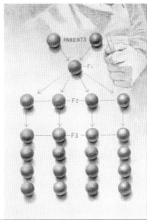

Slide #_____

What is one reason why Mendel used pea plants in his experiments?

What Are Genes?

What genes do

DNA

Genes are inherited

Field of study

Slide #_____

What do genes determine?

Genetics Today

What we learned from Mendel

Genes and heredity

Nongenetic factors that influence who we are

Slide #_____

Do we understand genetics and heredity completely today?

Gregor Mendel (1822–1884)

Early experiments with pea plants

Monestary
- Teacher
- Study at University of Vienna

Slide #_____

How are Mendel's principles referred to today?

Interest in How Heredity Works

Examples
- Crops
- Animals

Slide #_____

What example does the lecturer use to illustrate how heredity works in an animal?

SECOND LISTENING

Now that you have listened to the lecture once, listen to it again and take notes. Write on a separate piece of paper.

THIRD LISTENING

You will hear parts of the lecture again. Look through your notes as you listen. A notetaking mentor will discuss the notes. Circle the answer that is closest to the notes you took, and put a check (✓) next to the notes that the mentor wrote.

Part 1

1. a.

> Gs
> - in bd cells
> - md of DNA (=instrs for Gs)
> - inher'd
>   EX – hair col

b.

> Gs fnd in cells of bod
> md of deoksy___ ?
> instrs each cell supposd... ?
> Gs passd dn
> inher int trts frm grmoth/fath

Part 2

2. a.

> Mendel –intr – see rl man
> 1843 became monk
> 1851 – Univ Vien
> math & exper biol
> 2 yrs – left un.
> - nrvs tak exam
> - bcm famous sci

b.

> Mendel
> 1842 monk – teach
> 1851 Univ Vien – math & biol

c.

> Mendel

Part 3

3. a.

> Tm Knight – pea flwr exp:
>   viol fl X wh. fl = all v offspr (!)
>   BUT v X v offspr = v & w (!)
>   – w reapp – K cdnt expl

b.

> Tm Knight exp w/viol & wh pea flwrs
> 🌸V X 🌸w
>   ↓
> 1. all 🌸V (!)
> BUT 1. 🌸V X 🌸V
>   ↓
> 2. both 🌸V & 🌸w (!?– K)

🔊 ACCURACY CHECK
CD 4, TR 6

You will hear questions about the lecture. Answer each question by referring to the notes that you took while listening to the lecture.

1. a. our DNA
   b. how living creatures function
   c. everything about us

2. a. They are identical.
   b. They are unique to each person.
   c. Most are the same in all people.

3. a. They are completely different.
   b. Many are the same.
   c. They are 97 percent the same.

4. a. more than 200 years old
   b. less than 40 years old
   c. less than 200 years old

5. a. mathematics
   b. biology
   c. both a and b

6. a. Their inherited traits are predictable.
   b. They are always either violet or white.
   c. They reproduce very quickly.

7. a. to breed stronger animals
   b. to win races
   c. to grow wheat instead of corn

8. a. body weight
   b. eye color
   c. height

ORAL SUMMARY

Use your notes to create an oral summary of the lecture with a partner. As you work together, add details to your notes that your partner included but you had missed.

DISCUSSION

Discuss the following questions with a classmate or in a small group.

1. What evidence do you see for heredity in your family? Discuss physical and behavioral or intellectual traits.

2. The lecturer described Thomas Knight's experiments crossing plants with violet and white flowers, and pointed out his confusion when the white flowers reappeared in the second generation. Can you or any of your classmates explain why this happened? Review the experiment and discuss.

3. The lecturer states that most of what we know today about genetics has been learned in the past few decades. Why do you think this is true?

PRE-READING

The following Reading is about how genetic patterns can be traced through human history. Before you read, answer the following questions. Share your answers with a classmate.

1. Look at the picture of a cell below. Can you identify the different parts of the cell? Where are the genes?

2. Scan the article and locate the two subtitles. For each subtitle, write a question that you would like to have answered.

READING

Now read the article.

Genes and Population Genetics

The human body is made of some 50 to 100 trillion cells, which form the basic units of life and combine to form more complex tissues and organs. Inside each cell, genes comprise a "blueprint" for protein production that determines how the cell will function. Genes also determine physical traits. The complete set of some 20,000 to 25,000 genes is called the genome. Only a tiny fraction of the total genome sets the human body apart from those of other animals.

Most cells have similar basic structure. An outer layer, called the cell membrane, contains fluid called cytoplasm. Within the cytoplasm are many different specialized "little organs," called organelles. The most important of these is the nucleus, which controls the cell and houses the genetic material in structures called chromosomes. Another type of organelle is the mitochondria. These "cellular power plants" have their own genome, and do not recombine during reproduction.

During reproduction, each cell's DNA, which is in the form of a double helix, separates into two unique strands. The individual strands duplicate themselves for the next generation, but the process is not always perfect. Random "copying errors," or mutations, can and do occur along the genome's long spelling sequence of base pairs.

When mutations are passed down through the generations they become genetic markers of descent, forming a complex story that can be traced backward in time. The exact shape of this tree is also affected by natural selection and migration.

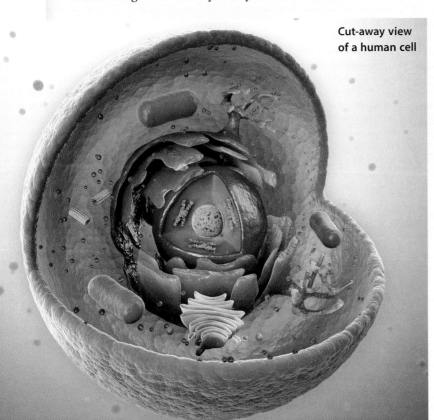

Cut-away view of a human cell

Natural selection

Natural selection is a process that favors beneficial genetic mutations and limits harmful ones. Organisms that possess an advantageous trait either attract mates more easily or survive in greater numbers. Such traits are passed on to increasingly larger numbers of individuals with each successive generation. The cumulative effect of natural selection produces populations that have evolved to succeed in their unique environments. This effect is readily seen in the physical diversity of plants, animal species, and human populations worldwide.

Migration

Y-chromosome DNA, passed from father to son, and mitochondrial DNA, passed from a mother to all her children, are varied through the generations only by occasional natural mutations, or genetic markers. These mutations, occurring in an otherwise continuous string of genetic replication, serve as genetic signposts for tracing human evolution. By following a marker back though time to its origin, geneticists can identify the most recent common ancestor of everyone alive who carries a given marker. The divergent branches of the human family tree, represented by groups carrying a particular genetic marker, can be followed back to "nodes" on the tree where a mutation split a branch into two directions. Eventually, these branches can be followed backward all the way to a common African root—a common ancestor of us all.

DISCUSSION

Discuss these questions with a classmate.

1. How much of the article was a review of what you heard in the lecture?

2. What information in the reading surprised you?

3. Compare the concepts of natural selection, discussed in the reading, with selective breeding, discussed in the lecture. How are they similar and how do they differ? Do humans always make good choices when they breed animals and plants?

RESEARCH PROJECT

Individually or in a group, research one of the following topics. Write a short paper on the topic, or plan and present a group presentation to inform the class about the topic.

1. Research the mechanism of recessive inheritance and try to find examples of recessive traits that you share with your grandparents and not your parents.

2. Choose an area of the world that has a distinctive physical environment and research its plant and animal species. Analyze how the species have adapted to their environment.

3. Choose another related topic that interests you or your group.

Genetic Engineering

Playing Roulette with Mother Nature's Designs?

TOPIC PREVIEW

Answer the following questions with a partner or your classmates.

1. Look at the title of this chapter. How do you think the term *playing roulette* relates to *genetic engineering*?

2. Discuss what you see in the photograph on this page. Why do you think this fish was developed?

3. What advantages and disadvantages does genetically engineered food present, in your opinion?

A biologist shows how genetic engineering enables growth in salmon.

VOCABULARY PREVIEW

CD 4, TR 7

A Read through the sentences below, which are missing vocabulary from the lecture. Listen to the sentences and write the missing words in the blanks.

1. I'll be touching on some of the important advances that have been made in recent years using genetic engineering, and also some of the _____ that have arisen.

2. The new DNA causes the _____ to function in a different way, and this function or trait can then be inherited by _____ generations.

3. One way to increase _____ is to make plants _____ to disease so that more of the crop survives and is harvested.

4. Transgenic Bt crops produce enough _____ to actually kill the harmful insect, so farmers don't need to spray their crops with _____.

5. If it is approved by the FDA—that's the U.S. government agency that _____ food—the genetically modified salmon would be the first genetically altered animal to be approved for human _____ in the United States.

6. The genetically altered fish has never been eaten before, and it could cause dangerous _____, especially because seafood tends to be quite _____.

7. _____ are concerned that the fish will escape and breed with the wild salmon population, which is already _____.

8. The FDA granted marketing approval for _____ goat antithrombin, the first drug to be produced in genetically modified _____.

9. _____ have questions about gene therapy.

10. How long will it be before we're _____—and maybe selecting— human _____ for characteristics such as physical strength?

B Check the spelling of the vocabulary words with your teacher. Discuss the meanings of these words and any other unfamiliar words in the sentences.

PREDICTIONS

Think about the questions in the Topic Preview on page 99 and the sentences you heard in the Vocabulary Preview. Write three questions that you think will be answered in the lecture. Share your questions with your classmates.

NOTETAKING PREPARATION

Vocabulary: Recovering Meaning as You Listen

When an unfamiliar word or expression is used in a lecture, the lecturer will often follow it with a synonym or a definition, using a signal word or phrase. For example:

> ..., or ...
> ..., that is, ...
> ...; in other words ...

The synonym or definition will usually follow a pause and echo the stress and intonation of the word being defined. The lecturer is "replaying" the information by substituting the definition in place of the unfamiliar word or expression. Sometimes a lecturer will pause before a synonym or a definition, but not use a signal word. For example:

> ... *the production of* pharmaceuticals [pause] drugs [pause] *by genetic engineering* ...

Be sure to pay attention to how an unfamiliar word is used in a sentence. You can usually learn enough of the meaning this way to follow the lecture.

Try not to spend time writing an unfamiliar word or expression. Just write the first letters and leave space with a question mark. Listen for a definition to put in the space. If you don't hear one, you can ask a classmate or the lecturer later.

A Read the phrases on the left, which contain words that may be unfamiliar. Draw a line to match each phrase on the left with a phrase on the right that explains it.

some controversies that have arisen, uh,	where the effect is on the body of only a particular individual
it develops a resistance to the toxin— in other words	specific concerns that some people have
This can be done in somatic cells, that is,	it takes more to kill it

CD 4, TR 8

B Listen to the sentences from the lecture, which contain explanations of the words and expressions below. Take brief notes showing the meaning of each word.

1. transgenic: _____

2. drought: _____

3. germ line cells: _____

4. cloning: _____

5. antithrombin: _____

FIRST LISTENING
CD 4, TR 9

Listen to the lecture and number the slides on this page and the next in the order they would be shown during the lecture. Write the number of the slide on the line provided and answer the question to the right of the slide.

Genetically Modified

Definition

Uses of genetic modification

In agriculture – GMOs
- examples
- main goal of GM

Slide #_____

What percent of the cotton grown in the United States is genetically modified?

Genetic Engineering

Definition
- advances
- concerns

Slide #_____

Name one of the fields in which genetic engineering has made great advances.

Genetic Modification (GM) in Agriculture

Main goal

Specific modifications
- examples

Concerns about GM

Slide #_____

What is the fastest growing area of agriculture today?

Gene Therapy and Human Genetic Engineering

Gene therapy
- in somatic cells or reproductive cells
- current uses

Ethical concerns: playing roulette with nature?

Slide #_____

How successful are the technology and use of gene therapy today?

Genetic Engineering in Medicine

Pharmaceuticals
- "pharming" defined
- examples

Animal models
- "knockout mouse"
- research on human diseases

Slide #_____

Name two human diseases for which mouse models have been developed.

SECOND LISTENING

CD 4, TR 10

Now that you have listened to the lecture once, listen to it again and take notes. Write on a separate piece of paper.

THIRD LISTENING

CD 4, TR 11

You will hear parts of the lecture again. Look through your notes as you listen. A notetaking mentor will discuss the notes. Circle the answer that is closest to the notes you took, and put a check (✓) next to the notes that the mentor wrote.

Part 1

1. a.

> Lect. prevu:
> Genet engin'rng
> • defn
> • imprt. rcnt advcs (agr & med)
> • ~~to~~ ppls' conc'ns ~~?~~
>   pract & ethic'l

b.

> Genet eng.
> • what is?
> • impor. advanc (rcnt)
> • concns
>   pract & ethicl
> Projcts: agr & medcn

Part 2

2. a.

> Why GMOs? ↗ fd prod – wrld pop ↗, agr land ↘
> How ↗ prod?
> GM → dz/insct resist
>   ex, Bt corn, potat, etc. Bt kills insct, dnt need spray. But PRBLM: Bt-resist – ex cotn India

b.

> Considr why modf fds & how
> • spcfc goals of GE in agr.
> • how GMOs achv goals or try
> • concerns
> Prim goal: ↑ fd prod (area ag ↓, wrld pop ↑)
> How? mk plnts dis & ins resist – ~~Basill~~
> BT – toxin kills bad inscts BUT org + toxin = resist to tox

Part 3

3. a.

> farmasu ..? pharming – genet eng
> = agric prod of ~~pharm...?~~ drugs
> gn mks drug – drg in host plnt / anim – plnt / anml mks drg
> If nd mr drg, clone tech to reprod
> EX –safflower – mks ins
> • transgen goat " antithro – prot – prevent bld clts

b.

> GE drugs ("pharming")
> 1. usfl drug-prod gn
> 2. put " in anml/plnt
> 3.   " prods drug
>   ↘ $$ thn in lab
>   nd ↗ drg? Clone plnt/anml
> EX: –saffl (oil) → insulin
>   –Xgen goat → antithrom__(?) – in mlk

104 Unit 5 · Biology

ACCURACY CHECK

CD 4, TR 12

You will hear questions about the lecture. Answer each question by referring to the notes that you took while listening to the lecture.

1. a. protein from another plant or animal
   b. DNA from another plant or animal
   c. toxins from another plant or animal

2. a. engineering
   b. medicine
   c. agriculture

3. a. to produce more food
   b. to produce healthier livestock
   c. to produce improved crops

4. a. goats
   b. soybeans
   c. sheep

5. a. They kill harmful insects.
   b. They tend to be less healthy.
   c. Insects develop resistance to them.

6. a. It may cause allergies.
   b. It may be toxic.
   c. Both *a.* and *b.*

7. a. tendency to be overweight
   b. immune deficiency
   c. mental depression

8. a. screening embryos
   b. treating disease
   c. determining eye or hair color

ORAL SUMMARY

Use your notes to create an oral summary of the lecture with your partner. As you work together, add details to your notes that your partner included but you had missed.

DISCUSSION

Discuss the following questions with a classmate or in a small group.

1. Do you know whether genetically modified foods are sold in your country? How do you feel about eating GM food products?

2. The lecturer mentions that critics of transgenic salmon refer to it as "Frankenfish." Discuss what this reference means. Do you agree with the critics? Why or why not?

3. The lecturer asks, "Are we playing roulette with Mother Nature?" Discuss what this means and give your opinion.

PRE-READING

The following Reading is about transgenic crops and animals. Before you read, answer the following questions. Share your answers with a classmate.

1. Look at the title of the article and the photograph on the next page. Write two things that you expect to learn about transgenic crops from the article.

2. In the lecture, the speaker presented some advantages and disadvantages associated with genetically modified organisms. Which are you interested in learning about more: advantages or disadvantages? Explain.

READING

Now read the article.

Food: How Altered?

In the brave new world of genetic engineering, Dean DellaPenna envisions this cornucopia: tomatoes and broccoli bursting with cancer-fighting chemicals and vitamin-enhanced crops of rice, sweet potatoes, and cassava to help nourish the poor. He sees wheat, soy, and peanuts free of allergens; bananas that deliver vaccines; and vegetable oils so loaded with therapeutic ingredients that doctors "prescribe" them for patients at risk for cancer and heart disease. A plant biochemist at Michigan State University, DellaPenna believes that genetically engineered foods are the key to the next wave of advances in agriculture and health.

While DellaPenna and many others see great potential in the products of this new biotechnology, some see uncertainty, even danger. In North America and Europe, the value and impact of genetically engineered food crops have become subjects of intense debate, provoking reactions from unbridled optimism to fervent political opposition.

Just what are genetically engineered foods, and who is eating them? What do we know about their benefits—and their risks? What effect might engineered plants have on the environment and on agricultural practices around the world? Can they help solve the problem of feeding and preserving the health of the Earth's burgeoning population?

Most people in the United States don't realize that they've been eating genetically engineered foods since the mid-1990s. And in fact, genetic modification is much older than that. Humans have been altering the genetic makeup of plants for millennia, keeping seeds from the best crops and planting them in following years, breeding and crossbreeding varieties to make them taste sweeter, grow bigger, last longer. But the technique of genetic engineering is new and quite different from conventional breeding. Traditional breeders cross-related organisms whose genetic makeups are similar. In so doing, they transfer tens of thousands of genes. By contrast, today's genetic engineers can transfer just a few genes at a time between species that are distantly related or not related at all.

The engineered organisms produced by transferring genes between species are referred to as "transgenic." Several dozen transgenic food crops are currently on the market, among them varieties of corn, squash, canola, soybeans, and cotton, from which cottonseed oil is produced. Most of these crops are engineered to help farmers deal with age-old agriculture problems: weeds, insects, and disease.

With the new tools of genetic engineering, scientists have also created transgenic animals. Atlantic salmon grow more slowly during the winter, but

Researcher monitoring modified plant cell growth in specimen dishes

Whether biotech foods will deliver on their promise of eliminating world hunger and bettering the lives of all remains to be seen. Their potential is enormous, yet they carry risks—and we may pay for accidents or errors in judgment in ways we cannot yet imagine. But the biggest mistake of all would be to blindly reject or endorse this new technology. If we analyze carefully how, where, and why we introduce genetically altered products, and if we test them thoroughly and judge them wisely, we can weigh their risks against their benefits to those who need them most.

engineered salmon, "improved" by the insertion of modified growth-hormone genes from other fish, reach market size in about half the normal time [see the photo on page 99]. These transgenic salmon have not yet entered the market.

DISCUSSION

Discuss these questions with a classmate.

1. What is Dean DellaPenna's attitude about genetically modified organisms (GMOs)? How does his attitude compare with that of the lecturer?

2. How would you compare the attitudes of the author and the lecturer toward GMOs? Support your opinion.

3. What did you learn from the article that you didn't hear in the lecture?

RESEARCH PROJECT

Individually or in a group, research one of the following topics. Write a short paper on the topic, or plan and present a group presentation to inform the class about the topic.

1. Labeling of GM food products: What laws exist in the United States? In other countries?

2. Animal models of human diseases: What diseases are being researched today? Is progress being made?

3. Genetically modified salmon: At the time this lecture was given, the U.S. FDA had not yet approved the sale of GM salmon. Has that changed? Is GM salmon still controversial?

4. Gene therapy: What recent advances (if any) have been made? What risks are currently associated with gene therapy?

5. Choose another related topic that interests you or your group.

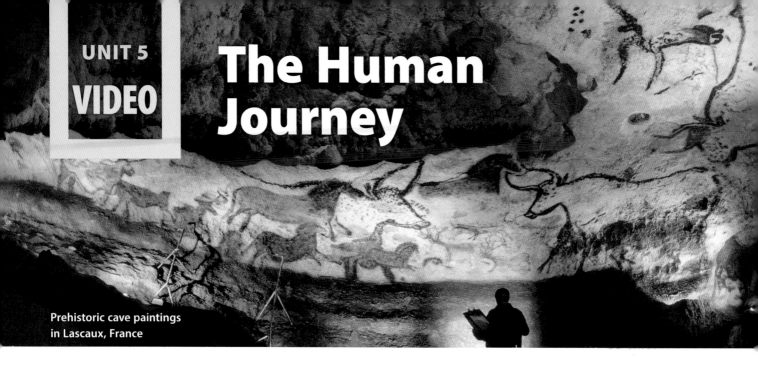

UNIT 5
VIDEO

The Human Journey

Prehistoric cave paintings in Lascaux, France

TOPIC PREVIEW

Fill in your family tree below. Then talk with a partner about what physical traits, such as eye color or height, and personality traits, such as shyness or friendliness, you have inherited from different members of your family.

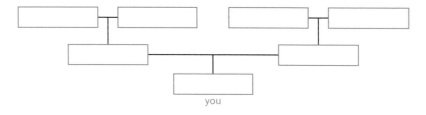

you

VOCABULARY PREVIEW

A Read the definitions of these key words and phrases that you will hear during the video.

spring from come from

paleoanthropology the study of ancient humans, primarily through fossils

direct lines of descent series of people born in a family going back through time from parent to child

ancestry relationships to people going back many generations into the past

genealogy the study of family history and relationships back through many generations

trace back follow back in time or place

pass it on to their children give their children the same DNA or genes as they have

lineages members of one's family going back through history from parent to child

maternal relating to a mother

paternal relating to a father

B **Work with a partner and discuss answers to the following questions.**

1. Are you interested in **genealogy**? How far can you **trace back** your family?

2. What is something that you would like to **pass on to your children**?

3. What sorts of things do you think a **paleoanthropologist** can discover?

4. Who in your culture comes from a famous **lineage**, in other words, they can trace their **line of descent** back to someone famous?

5. Do you have any famous **ancestry**?

6. Have you ever heard the idea that humans **spring from** aliens who visited this planet millions of years ago? What do you think of this idea?

7. What do you know about your **paternal** and **maternal** grandparents?

VIEWING

🖥 FIRST VIEWING

Watch the video, and then compare your first impressions with a partner. Talk about what you remember, what surprised you, and what interested you.

🖥 SECOND VIEWING

Watch the video again. Listen for the missing words and write them in the blanks.

1. Well, historically, these questions have been approached through the study of stones and _____ .

2. In our DNA, inside of nearly every cell in our body, DNA that we've _____ from those parents, grandparents, great-grandparents and so on, and this traces an unbroken line of descent going back in _____ .

3. So if you have mitochondrial DNA, which everyone in the room does, you got it from your _____, and she got it from her _____ .

4. By looking at the pattern of these genetic variants, these random _____ that have occurred over time, on both of these lineages, we can construct family _____ for everybody alive today.

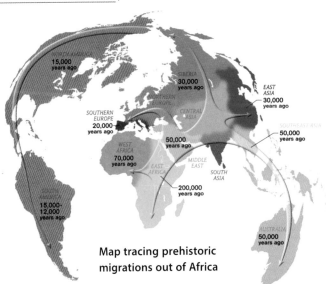

Map tracing prehistoric migrations out of Africa

Complete these notes as you watch the video. Use abbreviations and symbols.

RQs = How expl patterns of _____ ?

= Are we all _____ ?

= Why occ all _____ ?

1) Poss answ

a) study of _____

  – but only leads to poss ≠ probs.

b) genetics → _____

2) Genetics vs geneology

a) gen'logy → brick wall

b) DNA can trace _____

3) We can study

a) mitochondrial DNA _____

b) Y-chromosome from _____

c) genetic variants

  → _____

AFTER VIEWING

ORAL SUMMARY

Use your notes to create an oral summary of the video with your partner. As you work together, add details to your notes that your partner included but you had missed.

DISCUSSION

Discuss the following questions with a classmate or in a small group.

1. How does studying history through paleoanthropology and archaeology differ from Spencer Wells' approach as a geneticist?

2. Spencer Wells says "it turns out there is a written document in effect, that we're all carrying around inside of ourselves." What does he mean by this?

3. What do you know about how scientists' understanding of DNA has influenced the fields of agriculture, medicine, and crime fighting?

Videoscripts

The Gift of Traveling

Our kids have traveled to every continent except Antarctica. More importantly, when we travel they have lived in communities. We never stayed in hotels. And so they were always in little communities where they were hanging out with kids. And sometimes they had language in common, and many times they did not. And they've learned how to have fun the way those kids had fun.

And they're very confident travelers. Our daughter— you know, she's 18 now and she has no problem hopping on a plane and going overseas. And it is not a stressful thing for her. She really is excited about it and remembers all of our trips with, you know, enthusiasm and great memories. So, and I think they also—our kids—I think our kids also understand that people all over the world are different, that you don't assume that they are going to be the same as we are. But that if you go into each culture open and look people in the eye and observe and listen, you're going to make connections that are well beyond what most travelers get to see. And I think what I've learned from my kids is how delightful flexibility is and how naturally flexible most kids are, as long as they've got the basics. You know, food and sleep and a little something to keep them entertained. They pretty much can set up camp anywhere.

Almost everything's been photographed. And so the real challenge for a photographer is to bring her or his own unique vision to that subject matter. And in the case of the work that I do on assignment, it's primarily telling a story that is compelling enough—where you know the photograph is compelling enough to get people interested in reading the captions or what's going on. And hopefully that will lead them into a more in-depth written piece.

What traveling has taught me is that once, you know, step into another culture and you allow yourself to really immerse yourself in another culture and be available to them, communication happens very quickly. And it doesn't require perfect language skills. It doesn't require introductions. It's really something that happens when you are your honest self, when you recognize that you are a guest in another culture and that you really need to listen to people on a different level and abide by their way of doing things. That's the best part of travel for me. In fact, it's kind of spoiled regular travel for me because the camera has always given me an opportunity to walk up to people and spend time with them and even go home with them.

I think one of the most inspirational parts about photography is that you're never done. You're always growing, and when you travel you're always learning. So to have a career where I get to be creative, I'm immersed in really interesting situations, and I continue to grow artistically. What's better than that?

Palenque

George Stuart: Hello there. It's good to be back. As you can see from this wonderful photograph, the site itself—Palenque—sits on a kind of a shelf. The place sits in Chiapas, down here in the Maya area. And there's Palenque right there. Archaeology came to Palenque in 1934. When Mexico formed its National Institute of Anthropology and History, they sent Miguel Angel Fernandez there to start digging the palace.

When they finished the palace, they started looking over the temple and the inscriptions. This was how it was in 1942, and 1948, when Alberto Ruiz was hired to start. And he walked in the temple up there and he noticed something. And that is, that the floor of the temple was made out of big, stone slabs with holes in them. So Alberto had the workers pull up the stone. And underneath the stone there were two steps leading down. He didn't know whether it went down four more feet and stopped, or whether there were three steps. At the end of the summer of '48, he'd gone down 23 steps.

Finally, in June of 1952, he walked into this empty room at the bottom, and there was nothing there. And Juan Chablé, who was one of the masons, the head mason, said, "Don Alberto, there's a funny-looking, little triangular stone over there against the wall, if we could move that, I'll bet you there's something behind it." So they moved the triangular stone aside, and there was a room—a room with a stone in it. He thought it was an altar, a table. He didn't know what it was; nobody had ever found anything like that. And then he came back and Juan Chablé, the mason, said, "Hey, Don Alberto, why don't you drill a hole in the side of this thing and see if it's hollow?" He did, and it was. We went into town and got 15 automobile jacks and pulled the thing up, and there was a body inside. And so what I'm going to do is let David take the story here for a while and talk about the man in the tomb.

David Stuart: Okay, we're going to shift gears a little bit and look at a lot of detail at what turned out to be, I guess, the American equivalent—if there is one—to King Tut's tomb. His full name was K'inich Janaab' Pakal, and he was the greatest king of Palenque, one of the greatest of all Maya kings. Now, Pakal was born in the year 603 AD. We know from the inscriptions. He came to power in 615. So he was 12 years old when he became king. This is an early photograph of Pakal himself, in his tomb, after the inner slab was lifted. He was covered in jade, as a good Maya king would be. A jade collar, jade bracelets, and an extraordinary mask as well.

Here is Pakal. What you're seeing here, of course, is some of the jade and the mask. Unbelievable.

Years and years after he's dead, Pakal is still at the center of everything. And this is why I think Palenque—what we, most of what we see of Palenque in that central area—is Pakal City. It's just an incredible place to be, and it will always have that aura about it, I hope.

UNIT 3 VIDEO

An Actor and a Travel Writer

Interviewer: How did acting enter your life? How did you become an actor? How did you get started?

McCarthy: Good grief. I had just gotten cut from the high school basketball team and I was moping around the house, and my mother said, "Why don't you go try out for the play, dear?" I'm like, "I don't want to be in a play." And so I did, and that experience, I have to say, changed my life. My life suddenly made sense to me in a way it hadn't before. I felt like I belonged in a way I'd never experienced before. I felt powerful, seen, and I wanted to be seen. Whereas opposed to before that I'd been very reticent and shy. And I knew it was important because I told no one. I told . . . I didn't tell anyone how important . . . , "Yea, yea, it was good. I liked it, yea. When's the next one?" And so then I went to college for acting, and I took it more seriously, and it took me more seriously. And after two years of college, I was kicked out of college and got a job as an actor. And then it sort of happened very quickly for me. So that's how it began.

Interviewer: And then one role led to another led to another?

McCarthy: Well, then I didn't work for a year, and then I got a job as the Burger King boy in a commercial. No, I was the Pepsi boy in the Burger King commercial. And so that supported me for a few years, that commercial. And

then I got another job. And then suddenly I got jobs very quickly, and I was suddenly a 22-year-old star.

Interviewer: So how did travel writing enter this equation?

McCarthy: It entered because at a certain point in my life, when I was about 30, I looked up and said, "Huh?" So I started reading a lot of travel literature, and I thought it was a very interesting genre, you know. So, I just started traveling. I just started buying tickets to places, you know buy a ticket into Cape Town and out of Dar es Salaam two months later. And the rest I'd just fill in. Or I'd go to Southeast Asia and just go for a while. And so every year I would, you know, take a couple months and do that. And I started just sort of writing little things. I wasn't keeping a journal in any way, but I would write little scenes of encounters I had with people. Just for myself, I'd write just sort of a scene . . . because that's what I knew how to do, was be in scenes. So I'd write the scene between me and the kid who picked me up, you know, on the moped in Hanoi and took me around for the day. And I would write that scene. I did nothing with them. I sat them in a drawer.

Interviewer: When you look at your life do you feel like you're more an actor, or a travel writer?

McCarthy: I'm just a guy, I don't know, I don't, I don't think of it that way. My life's sort of transitioning, you know. I'll always be the guy who was in *Pretty in Pink*, you know? I mean so that's okay, you know. Hopefully I'll be in some other things, too, you know, but that's certainly part of who I am. You know I wouldn't be here, sitting here, if I wasn't in those movies. You know what I mean? I may be a travel writer . . . you wouldn't be talking to just some travel writer. You know what I mean? So it's given me opportunities and opened doors for me and, you know, so it's just part of my story.

Interviewer: Well, thank you, Andrew, for a really, really delightful evening. Thank you very much.

UNIT 4 VIDEO

Digital Nomad

So, on New Year's Day, I head out from this very building, National Geographic Headquarters. It was symbolic. I wanted to show that I was just like these explorers who were sent out by the *Geographic* to go explore the world. And I was going to start from this very point on earth, and I was going to go to the bottom of the world. And I just got to the bus station on the S2 bus, which runs just outside Sixteenth Street, and I paid my fare, which was $1.35, and I got on the bus and took off. And here I am sending my first Tweet, a real-time narrative.

Now, this was an experiment for me, because all of the original explorers would go and they would keep a journal, and they would write about their trip, and then they would come home and actually write a book and publish. And this was a past tense kind of memoir about their journey. Well, I wanted to do this same thing, but I wanted to do it in real time. I just wanted to write the story as it was happening.

And I learned something, because I sent over 5,000 Tweets when I traveled from Washington, D.C., to Antarctica. And I learned that there was a more effective way to write on Twitter and a less effective. And for those who don't know Twitter, you know it's a way to share by text message. You're limited to 140 characters so you have to keep it really short. But you can say so much if you do it right. Now, I didn't start out as a pro. I'm still not a pro, but I'm learning, and I learned a lot from poets. This is one of my favorite poems by Jack Kerouac. It's from his American haiku, written in 1959: "Nightfall, boy smashing dandelions with a stick." Now, this follows an ancient Japanese form of poetry. But it's very short and it has all the great ingredients of a Tweet, of storytelling. He has set the stage. He's given you time. He's given you place. He's given you color. He's given you a character. And he's given you action. And you need all of these things when you're writing Twitter.

I've Tweeted from hot-air balloons. I've Tweeted from birchbark canoes. I've Tweeted above Niagara Falls in a helicopter. I've Tweeted from camelbacks. And I've Tweeted—not underwater, that doesn't work yet, but almost. I Tweeted in real time while flying a plane, in French.

Now I just want to leave with a couple of little tips for all of you digital nomads out there, things that I've learned that have helped me. One, besides being there, which is very important, always be there. Never let the experience of, you know, never let sharing the experience eclipse having the experience. And that's very possible. You can walk into any coffee shop here and you're going to see a million people with their phones, looking down like this. And it's very hard to experience the world around you when you're doing this.

This is in Botswana, in the Okavango Delta, beautiful place surrounded by wildlife, and I was with two journalists from New York. And we're out there, surrounded by lions, and all they cared about was that there was no reception on their phone. And there was one spot by the river near the Namibian border where there was a wildebeest carcass. And they always wanted to drive by the carcass, because the carcass, for whatever reason, had coverage. So they could always download their e-mail and their Tweets whenever we got by the carcass. So they were always like, "Let's go to the carcass, let's go to the carcass." And they were so obsessed with that, they missed out everything else that we were around. And if you're so obsessed with kind of sharing the experience, you miss the things that are around you.

There's one fourth tip that I have and I'll close with this. And that is, you have to unplug periodically. And if you don't, you just become crazed because the human mind works very different than our digital technology. Our minds are fascinating. We have subconsciouses that are always working. We take much better pictures than cameras do. We feel a place. We have these emotions. But if we don't shut off, we're not able to process that and share it. So, I'll just leave with that. You should unplug. You will sleep much better if you do. And I want to thank all of you for coming tonight and listening to my stories. Really grateful.

UNIT 5 VIDEO

The Human Journey

We have a huge amount of diversity as a species. We travel the world, walk down the street in a major city like Washington or New York, and we see people who seem to be so different from each other and from ourselves. We as population geneticists are trying to address the question of, well, you know, what is it that led to us being so successful and how do we explain these patterns of diversity that we see when we look around the world? Are we in fact all related to each other, and if so, how closely? And the other question is one of journey. If we do spring from a common source, as a species, how do we come to occupy every corner of the globe, in the process, generating these patterns of diversity that we see today in all seven billion of us and growing?

Well, historically, these questions have been approached through the study of stones and bones, often the field of paleoanthropology, and of course archaeology, its sister science—going out and digging things up out of the ground and guessing at how they may relate to individuals living in the present. The problem is, I would like to suggest as a geneticist, while the field of paleoanthropology, and the field of archaeology as well, give us certain insights into our past, possibilities about origins and journeys of the people alive today, they don't give us the probabilities about direct lines of descent that we really want . . . possibilities about our ancestry but not the probabilities that we're looking for as scientists.

We as geneticists take a slightly different approach. We start in the present and we work our back into the past. We take a genealogical approach. It's, in effect, like building a family tree . . . a family tree for everybody alive today. Now, genealogy is currently the second most popular hobby in the United States, after gardening and

I think it's poised to overtake gardening very soon. Now the problem is, everybody who's ever tried to construct a family tree eventually hits what we call a *brick wall* in the genealogical community—a point beyond which there is no written record. And beyond that point we simply enter this dark and mysterious realm we call history and ultimately, prehistory. But it turns out there is a written document in effect, that we're all carrying around inside of ourselves. In our DNA, inside of nearly every cell in our body, DNA that we've inherited from those parents, grandparents, great-grandparents, and so on, and this traces an unbroken line of descent going back in time. This is what allows us to trace back to the very earliest days of our species, allowing this global genealogical approach to the study of human history.

So by looking at people from all over the world, asking, in effect, a very open-ended scientific question: What is the pattern of human variation that we see today, globally? Looking in particular at two pieces of DNA that are proven to be incredibly valuable in the study of human origins and migrations. Mitochondrial DNA—mtDNA, which traces a purely maternal line of descent:

Women pass it on to their children, everybody has it but only women pass it on. So if you have mitochondrial DNA, which everyone in the room does, you got it from your mom and she got it from her mom, and she got it from her mom. So it tells you about mother's, mother's, mother's, mother's mother, back to the very first mother.

There is an equivalent piece of DNA on the male side, in fact the chunk of DNA, the little chromosome as we call it, the Y-chromosome that makes men, men. But basically it traces a purely paternal line of descent, an unbroken line of descent going back in time. Sons inherit it from their fathers; they got it from their fathers, and so on—the Y-chromosome. By looking at the pattern of these genetic variants, these random changes that have occurred over time, on both of these lineages, we can construct family trees for everybody alive today.

It's a fascinating way of approaching the study of human history, because we, as people who study primarily modern human lineages, are getting only a glimpse of the actual process that went on to create that. So it's a huge addition to our understanding of the past.

Acknowledgments

62: Excerpt from "Why are Young, Educated Americans Going Back to the Farm" by Nelson Harvey, from Turnstyle/Youth Radio, September 21, 2011. Copyright © 2011 by Youth Radio. Reprinted by permission.
75: Excerpt from "Love that Lingua Franca" by Diasann McLane from *National Geographic Traveler*, September, 2011. Reprinted by permission of the National Geographic Society. All rights reserved.

Sources

9: "Vikings Filed Their Teeth, Skeleton Study Shows," National Geographic News, February 3, 2006, **18:** "Last of the Cave People," *National Geographic*, February, 2012 **31:** "Ramses the Great," *National Geographic*, April, 1991, **40:** "Terra-Cotta Army Protects First Emperor's Tomb," NationalGeographic.com, **53:** "'Second Life,' Other Virtual Worlds Reshaping Human Interaction," National Geographic News, October 17, 2006, **84:** "Smarter Teams Are More Sensitive, Have More Women?" National Geographic News, September 30, 2010, **97:** "The Genographic Project," NationalGeographic.com, **106:** "Food: How Altered?" *National Geographic*, May, 2002.

Images

Inside front cover: William Allen/National Geogrpahic Stock, Kenneth Garrett/National Geographic Stock, Jeffrey Ufberg/WireImage Collection/Getty Images, Courtesy of Andrew Evans, Mark Thiessen/National Geographic Stock, **1:** Jill Schneider/National Geographic Stock, **2–3:** Kenneth Garrett/National Geographic Stock, **5:** Kenneth Garrett/National Geographic Stock, **6:** Tim Laman/National Geographic Stock, **6:** New York Public Library/Photo Researchers Collection/Getty Images, **9:** Staffan Hyll, **10:** Peter Essick/National Geographic Stock, **11:** Roy Toft/National Geographic Stock, **14:** James P. Blair/National Geographic Stock, **14:** James P. Blair/National Geographic Stock, **15:** Nicole Duplaix/Peter Arnold Collection/Getty Images, **15:** Frans Lanting/National Geographic Stock, **19:** Amy Toensing/National Geographic Stock, **20–21:** Annie Griffiths/National Geographic Stock, **21:** Annie Griffiths/National Geographic Stock, **23:** Kenneth Garrett/ National Geographic Stock, **24–25:** Kenneth Garrett/National Geographic Stock, **24:** Martin Gray/National Geographic Stock, **27:** Richard Nowitz/National Geographic Stock, **27:** Martin Gray/National Geographic Stock, **28:** Taylor S. Kennedy/National Geographic Stock, **28:** Kenneth Garrett/National Geographic Stock, **31:** O. Louis Mazzatenta/National Geographic Stock, **32:** O. Louis Mazzatenta/National Geographic Stock, **33:** Ira Block/National Geographic Stock, **36:** Raymond Gehman/National Geographic Stock, **36:** O.: Louis Mazzatenta/National Geographic Stock, **37:** O. Louis Mazzatenta/National Geographic Stock, **41:** O. Louis Mazzatenta/National Geographic Stock, **42–43:** Stephen Alvarez/National Geographic Stock, **43:** Kenneth Garrett/National Geographic Stock, **45:** Ola Dusegard/E+ Collection/Getty Images, **46:** Pete Mcbride/ National Geographic Stock, **47:** © creative soul - Fotolia.com, **49:** Richard Nowitz/National Geographic Stock, **50:** Klaus Vedfelt/Riser Collection/Getty Images, **50:** Asimetrica Juniper/Flickr Collection/Getty Images, **50:** © morganimation - Fotolia.com, **53:** The Washington Post/Getty Images, **54:** © Nmedia - Fotolia.com, **55:** Suzailan Shoroyo/National Geographic My Shot/National Geographic Stock, **58:** Derek Latta/E+ Collection/ Getty Images, **59:** Arthur Pollock/America 24-7 Collection/Getty Images, **59:** © Picture-Factory - Fotolia. com, **62:** Robert Kneschke/Shutterstock, **64–65:** Rob Lang/Taxi Collection/Getty Images, **65:** Jeffrey Ufberg/ WireImage Collection/Getty Images, **67:** Raul Touzon/National Geographic Stock, **68–69:** Raul Touzon/ National Geographic Stock, **71:** Flying Colours Ltd/Digital Vision Collection/Getty Images, **71:** © Jasmin Merdan - Fotolia.com, **72:** DAJ/Getty Images, **72:** Erik Dreyer/Stone Collection/Getty Images, **75:** PhotoTalk/ E+ Collection/Getty Images, **76:** © pink candy - Fotolia.com, **77:** Henrik Sorensen/Stone Collection/Getty Images, **80:** Lawrence Migdale/Photo Researchers Collection/Getty Images, **81:** © auremar - Fotolia.com, **81:** © auremar - Fotolia.com, **81:** © berc - Fotolia.com, **81:** Lane Oatey/Blue Jean Images/Getty Images, **84:** Marcin Balcerzak/Shutterstock, **86–87:** Beverly Joubert/National Geographic Stock, **87:** Beverly Joubert/ National Geographic Stock, **89:** Adrian Neal/Lifesize Collection/Getty Images, **90:** Ned M. Seidler/National Geographic Stock, **90–91:** © Gala_K - Fotolia.com, **93:** Ned M. Seidler/National Geographic Stock, **93:** David Sacks/Lifesize Collection/Getty Images, **94:** Pantheon / Superstock, **94:** Melissa Farlow/National Geographic Stock, **97:** © Mopic - Fotolia.com, **98:** Joe Stancampiano/National Geographic Stock, **99:** Jim Richardson/